ERIC SLOANE'S WEATHER BOOK

Also by Eric Sloane

Eric Sloane's
WEATHER
BOOK

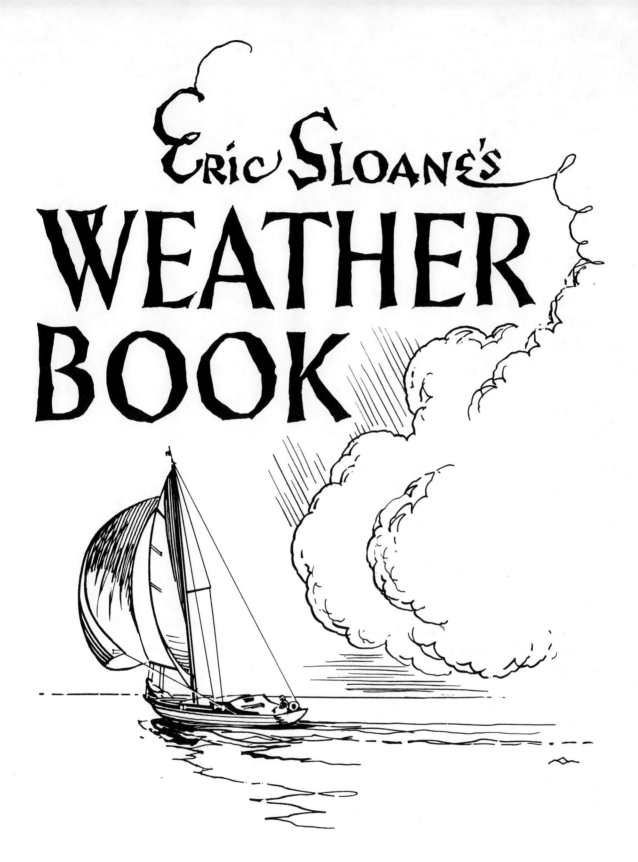

HAWTHORN/DUTTON
New York

10 11 12 13 14 15 16 17 18 19 20

AUTHOR'S NOTE

I wish I could write with ease. But every time I am asked to say something, I find myself drawing diagrams. Apparently I am not able to explain anything without making a picture. As a result, there are plenty of pictures in this book, so that if the old saying about a picture being worth a thousand words is true, this weather book ought to be worth while.

Recently, while designing the Hall of Atmosphere for the American Museum of Natural History (the Willetts Memorial), I found that a working model is probably worth a thousand pictures. I am grateful to Mr. William P. Willetts, who labored with me on that project in his converted squash court in Roslyn, Long Island; many of the ideas in this book evolved from my designing the museum display, and United States Navy models in his unusual workshop.

Air is funny stuff — it's so invisible. I have always thought that there should be some way of making pictures of the atmosphere to enable us humans, who are the poor fish swimming in that atmosphere, to *see the air*. It can't be done with mere words. To do the job, I tried to combine words and pictures in a series of weather articles, and as sailing men seem to be the most weather-wise among us, I sold them to *Rudder*. Mr. Boris Leonardi, the editor of that fine magazine, was so bombarded by readers asking that the series be put into book form that I decided to do something about it. That is the background of this *Weather Book*. I might add that, since the appearance of the *Rudder* articles, I have been most emphatically reminded that, if sailors *want* to be weather-wise, fliers *have* to be weather-wise, and *Flying Magazine* has asked that the material in these weather articles be presented in a form that will be interesting and helpful to the aviation world.

A few years ago I decided to become a painter and to paint only the sky and clouds. My idea was twofold. First, I can truthfully say that nothing during my life has impressed me so much as the sky. It is my religion and my philosophy. It is my cathedral, and I believe it to be a source of inspiration to anyone who wants to look upward. It is the only part of this world that Man will not change, because he cannot.

My second reason for becoming a sky artist was to make a living. Many of us, particularly the artists, ignore the sky. Museums are full of paintings with three quarters of their space devoted to sky, and yet art classes and books, which tell how to paint cats and dogs and trees and other things, never mention how to paint the sky and the clouds. I tried to fill that gap in a book entitled *Skies and the Artist*.

Before I attempted painting clouds I felt that I should study their anatomy. There is little written about the sky nowadays that is not technical, yet there are so many wonders to be seen in the heavens that I began to keep a sketchbook of weather phenomena just to explain to weather-minded friends what I had learned. This new book is for all friendly weather-minded readers—for the old-timer who sits on a porch rocker at sunset reading tomorrow's weather in the sky, for the sailor who can't tell the names of the clouds but knows them all like days in the week, for the beginner and the student bitten by the sky bug, and for all good people who marvel at the daily panorama of what goes on overhead.

CONTENTS

ERIC SLOANE'S WEATHER BOOK

Weather Sayings of the old Sailors

DEW INDICATES A GOOD DAY AHEAD: A DRY MORNING IS SIGN OF SHOWERS.

DISTANT SHORES LOOM UP "NEARER" BEFORE RAIN BECAUSE OF THINNING OF THE AIR.

LARGE HALO AROUND THE MOON INDICATES CIRRUS CLOUDFORM & WARM FRONT RAIN.

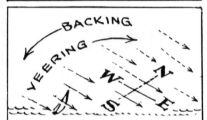

A VEERING WIND IS SIGN OF FAIR WEATHER: BACKING WIND MEANS RAIN.

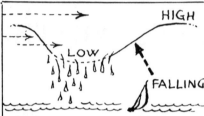

FALLING BAROMETER INDICATES NEARING "LOW" AREA, WITH WINDS AND RAIN.

RAIN IS MOST FREQUENT AT THE TURN OF THE TIDE (IF AIR IS HUMID)

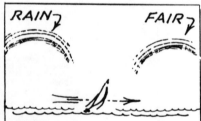

RAINBOW TO WINDWARD, RAIN AHEAD. RAINBOW TO LEEWARD, RAINS END.

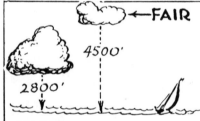

HIGHER THE CLOUDS, FINER THE WEATHER. LOWERING CEILINGS FORETELL A RAIN.

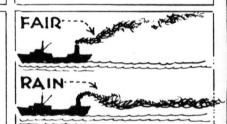

SMOKE THAT CURLS DOWNWARD AND LINGERS, MEANS A NEARING STORM.

THINNING AIR IS HARDER TO FLY IN. BIRDS "SIT IT OUT" BEFORE A STORM

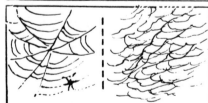

SKY FULL OF WEBBY CIRRUS FORETELLS DISTURBANCE AND RAINS ON ITS WAY

LIGHTNING FROM THE W. OR N.W. WILL REACH YOU; FROM S. OR S.E WILL PASS

Eric Sloane

Drawing 1

1 THE HUMAN SIDE OF THE WEATHER

The weather is with us wherever we are, yet nothing is more taken for granted than the daily drama of the sky.

The heavens are a fairyland, filled with marvels, to anyone who opens his mind and spirit to them; facts are often as inspiring as fancies and what one sees aloft in the skies is as real as anything to be experienced on earth.

Our heads are often bowed down with the material burdens of life, but we know that all through the ages thinking people have found time to look upward and to seek peace and solace in the panorama of weather. Emerson called the sky the daily bread of his eyes. Ruskin called it almost human in its passions, almost spiritual in its tenderness, almost divine in its infinity. Lincoln said he could not imagine a man looking up at the sky and denying God. These spiritual qualities of weather frequently outweigh the adverse influences that rain and snow have on our daily lives. They are, to my way of thinking, important enough to be a part of any book about the weather.

This book may help the reader to learn how to forecast tomorrow's weather; more important, it is hoped the book will give to many a new concept of weather, that it will explain the character as well as the mechanics of the sky and the atmosphere. Not everyone can be a meteorologist; but it is easy to be weather-wise, and the pleasure of being close to the weather is endless.

Anyone who has known a sailor with "a weather eye" and who has also seen the inside of a weather bureau knows the difference between being weather-wise and being meteorologically accurate. The meteorologist is a slave to the barrage of weather-map material and mathematical data that bombards him from all over the world and keeps him from looking out of the window at the sky. On the other hand, a man with a weather eye wears his badge of wisdom gracefully; he has a ready alertness to cloud changes or he has the calm assurance that tonight's rain will give way to a week of good weather. He has the gift of the upward glance, and his sky philosophy makes him a richer person.

Many meteorologists, I feel sure, began their lifework as sensitive children who responded to the thrill of clouds and wind, who were awed by thunder and lightning. Once I, too, thought that research into atmospheric phenomena would be as exciting as a flight to the stars in a space ship. But, alas, the disappointment of finding that weather books were filled with Latin names and graphs and algebraic equations was so great that it threatened to take the romance out of the skies forever for this weather student.

The unscientific-looking picture, Drawing 1, will serve to set the pattern of this book of observations and sketches on the weather. Perhaps the views and findings presented here will provoke the wrath of some of the old-school meteorologists; but the purpose is to arouse the

3

interest of the newly weather-wise. This weather lore may not be infallible, but it will be interesting for the reader to match it up with official weather forecasts and to try it out. Official forecasts, remember, are protected by very indefinite modifiers such as "probable," "possible," "fair," and "mild," while folklore about the weather usually comes straight out with "rainy," "windy," "clear," and so on.

Many of the weather sayings that have survived the years — those of the deceptive groundhog and goose-bone type — have never for a moment been accepted by men whose reason demands an adequate cause for every effect. But there are other weather sayings which remain always true.

In the course of modern living man has lost much of his weather wisdom. What with air conditioning and improved travel facilities, we seem to go where we want, and to do what we wish, regardless of the weather. Except for an occasional rained-out ball game or called-off sailing trip or postponed air flight, we presume that weather has very little influence upon us. But it has far more influence on us than is immediately apparent. We live in it, breathe it, actually swim through an atmospheric sea from room to room and from place to place; the slightest difference in the composition of this sea would change our way of living within a fraction of a second. No developments of our

technological age can alter the fact that we are creatures of the atmosphere.

Our forefathers and the men of ancient times had no weather maps, but they were, in the actual sense of the word, far more air-minded than we are.

Many people are surprised when it is pointed out that in Chapter 16 of Matthew there is a favorite of sailormen, a familiar weather saying first spoken by Christ: "When it is evening, ye say, It will be fair weather; for the sky is red. And in the morning, It will be foul weather today; for the sky is red and lowering." Few appear to be acquainted with that bit of weather lore in the Bible; but most of us know some version or other of the sailor's rhyme:

> *Red sky in the morning*
> *Is a sailor's sure warning;*
> *Red sky at night*
> *Is the sailor's delight.*

Folklore is generally frowned upon by scientific men, but many of its sayings and predictions have found scientific backing. The red sunset mentioned by Christ, for example, was a view of the sun through dust-laden air that would reach Him the next day. In most places, weather patterns tend to flow from west to east. If "tomorrow's air" lies westward as a mass of wet stuff, the sun shining through it appears to be a gray or yellowish disk, while, if this

Drawing 2

westward air is dry, the sun appears at its reddest.

Even scientific men are impressed by the accurate weather observations made by primitive people. Ancient Navajo blankets and pottery show cloud designs, with correct anvil tops and flat bottoms, as accurate as a trained meteorologist could devise today.

A few years ago a group of weathermen decided to test the accuracy of the legend about the caterpillar known to the early pioneers as the "Woolly Bear." The Woolly Bear was said to be an infallible prophet of winter weather — the wider his middle brown band, the milder the winter. The fact that scientific men put this bit of folklore to the test is significant, but the fact that the Woolly Bear is still forecasting winters with great accuracy is even more remarkable. (Drawing 2.)

Here is an old rhyme that is so crowded with weather lore evolved from accurate observation that the reader can almost feel the rain gathering and getting ready to come down:

SIGNS OF RAIN

The hollow winds begin to blow:
The clouds look black, the glass is low,
The soot falls down, the spaniels sleep,
And spiders from their cobwebs peep.
Last night the sun went pale to bed,
The moon in halos hid her head:
The walls are damp, the ditches smell,
Closed is the pink-eyed pimpernel.
Hark how the chairs and tables crack!
Old Betty's nerves are on the rack;
Loud quacks the duck, the peacocks cry,
The distant hills are seeming nigh.
Low o'er the grass the swallow wings,
The cricket, too, how sharp he sings!
Through the clear stream the fishes rise,
And nimbly catch incautious flies.
The glow-worms, numerous and light
Illumined the dewy dell last night;
And see yon rooks, how odd their flight!
They imitate the gliding kite,
And seem precipitate to fall,
As if they felt the piercing ball.
'Twill surely rain; I see with sorrow,
Our jaunt must be put off tomorrow.

All these signs and portents can be sensed and observed before a rainfall, and although the poet did not know the scientific explanation of them, he recognized them as reputable weather signs. Let us take the old rhyme apart meteorologically, line by line, and find the reasons behind its uncanny accuracy.

The hollow winds begin to blow refers to the hollowness of sound before a rain; this can be noticed particularly with boat horns, the droning of planes, and the hoot of train whistles, all of which seem unusually clear and as if sounded down a long corridor. This happens when the cloud ceiling and bad weather inversion lower to earth, the sounds then echoing back against the meteorological sounding board of the heavens. In fair weather, sound radiates outward and dissipates into clear space.

The clouds look black, the glass is low is elementary; dark clouds are dark because they hold more precipitation and because they reflect the darkness of a dull-colored earth, rather than refracting the light of the sun, as the ceiling of a weather front moves in. The "glass," meaning the barometer, will be discussed fully later.

The soot falls down indicates a lowering of air pressure: delicate soot is often kept in place within the chimney simply by the high pressure of good weather air; when the atmospheric pressure lowers (and the soot becomes heavy with humidity) chunks frequently fall into the fireplace below.

Last night the sun went pale to bed has already been commented upon in the explanation of Christ's words.

The moon in halos hid her head means that a mass of rain-bringing warm air has flowed in overhead, causing ice-crystal cloudform. When the sun or moon shines through ice-crystal clouds, a halo results.

The walls are damp, the ditches smell indicates humid air and a lessening of the atmospheric pressure that has held in much of the odor of swamps and wet places during the high pressure of good weather; when that pressure lowers, captive odors are released and things "smell more." Sailors who can "smell an

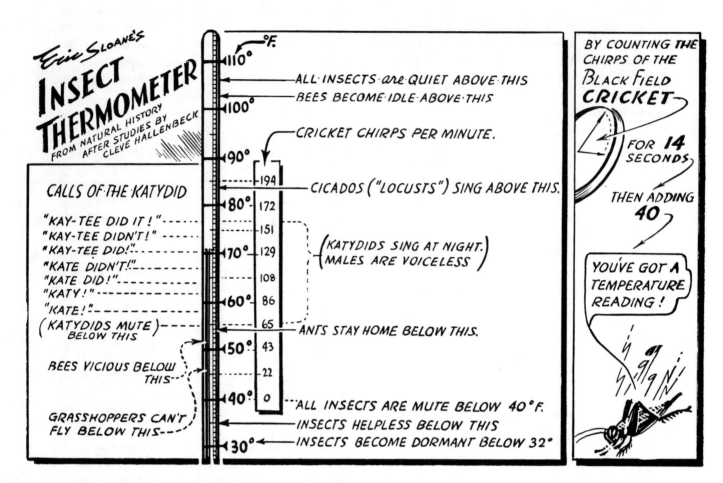

Drawing 3

approaching rain" really are simply sensitive to the odors of the floating seaweed and of tiny marine life that exudes captive smells when the barometric pressure lowers.

Hark how the chairs and tables crack hardly needs explanation, for we all know how wood "breathes," swelling and contracting with humidity and dryness.

But *Old Betty's nerves are on the rack* indicates more than the obvious mental depression of pre-storm atmosphere. A drop in air pressure affects the nerves instantly by causing greater dehydration of the tissues; old wounds begin to ache, corns and bunions are felt, the minute the barometer drops.

The distant hills are seeming nigh is an often-noticed weather sign of sailors. When the Connecticut shores appear unusually near to a Long

Islander, rain is usually less than a day away. Marine air is always rich with salt haze from evaporation during good weather, but becomes clear with the mixing action of unstable atmosphere. When the instability of pre-storm air invades the coast, the clearing-away of salt haze results in great visibility.

Low o'er the grass the swallow wings is a weather sign that to my knowledge has never been researched. Yet we know that bats and swallows have extremely sensitive ears which they use as a sort of radar mechanism during flight, to avoid hitting obstacles and to locate insects in the air. When pre-storm air pressure lowers abruptly, the pressure difference between the inside and outside of their heads becomes irritating, possibly painful. Therefore, bats and swallows will be seen seeking the relief of the highest pressure air, which of course is always found closest to the earth. When you see swallows flying so close to the water that their wings occasionally touch the surface, you may usually predict a lowering barometer and a rainy spell ahead. Likewise, very high-flying bats and swallows would foretell fine weather.

The cricket, too, how sharp he sings indicates that the old-timer observed the effect that weather has upon insects, especially crickets, which are astoundingly accurate atmospheric instruments. It has been recently learned that the cricket's reaction to temperature is often more immediate and accurate than that of the average thermometer, which has considerable lag and variation. If the chirps of the black cricket are counted for fourteen seconds and the number forty is then added to that figure, you will get the exact temperature of the air (where the cricket is) in degrees Fahrenheit. (Drawing 3.) You will also find the katydid a responsive insect-thermometer, its call lengthening with warmth, and shortening — and finally ending completely — with colder atmosphere.

Bird imitating *the gliding kite* would simply indicate an unstable condition in the atmosphere. Strong noonday thermals soon build into towering afternoon storm clouds, so that an unstable morning atmosphere might well indicate an afternoon shower. Also when the air

pressure lowers or the air becomes thin, birds must fly harder and faster in it in order to stay aloft; so much so, in fact, that before a hurricane or a stormy cyclonic atmosphere you will frequently find birds roosting or resting rather than staying aloft to face the strenuous flying conditions of the thinning air.

All these observations are of the kind that make being weather-wise a pleasure. When you know what they mean, they cease to be folklore weather prophecies and become science. For example, almost everyone has heard that "when the leaves show their backs" rain is on the way, and has probably thought that, if this be true, leaves of trees just naturally curl upward before a storm. Any schoolboy can explain that leaves are designed to grow in a pattern according to the prevailing good weather wind; therefore, a nonprevailing or stormy wind turns them over. It's that simple.

Today when we build a house we usually regard the land plot as flat, and we place our house ornamentally rather than meteorologically. The old houses were more often placed with great consideration for prevailing winds and sun exposure. A small hill or a grove of trees was not regarded only decoratively, as it is today, but as an atmospheric mechanism that insured the working of fireplaces, the elimination of mildew, freedom from snowdrifts and protection from unfavorable winds. The fact that many old barns still stand is a tribute to the air-mindedness of the pioneers who built them. You can usually remodel an old barn into a pleasant and comfortable home, but not even livestock could live well in some of our modern homes if they were remodeled into barns.

Actually a house is built not so much upon a piece of land as it is built upward into a section of atmosphere. The land surface that a house is set upon consists only of cellar and basement, but the larger portions of it — the sides and roof of the house — live in the weather. It makes sense, then, that the "air plot" or the "atmospheric acreage" is an important part of real estate which not only affects the construction of the home but also all the living that goes on

Drawing 4

within it. Drawing 4 shows a few of the values of placing a house correctly into its atmospheric acreage, as suggested by the early barn builders of New England and taken from early almanacs. An old builder's saying, "A house on a hill gets the air coming and going," is more scientific than it sounds, because warm daytime air is light and flows uphill, while night air flows downhill by its own dense weight. So a house halfway up a hill is assured of one complete daily ventilation, even in a dead calm.

Most people think of wood and other construction being protected if it is just kept dry or is covered from the elements. Yet sailors know that wooden boats last best if stored in free air and where the winter's salt spray is near; that seams open and rot when the wood dries out. They know the bad effects of stagnant air. Even cellars and underground airspaces require ventilation to protect them against damp-rot. Quite like human beings, old houses have "lived well" not by stagnating in pools of still air, but by "exercising" freely in the open. Sun-drawn, rain-swept, and settling each year a bit more comfortably on their foundations, they have watched new houses come and go in the sheltered valley or on the wrong side of the hill. This may sound more imaginative than scientific, but anyone who has ever felt the cheerfulness of an old house, or who has known the hard-to-explain unhappy mood of some real-estate Jonah, will know what I mean.

As far as I know, the effects of weather upon humans have been studied much too little; certainly they are not dealt with in any meteorological text. During the war, I did a manual for the Air Force which I called *Your Body in Flight;* it explained the effects of flying upon the human body, and much of the research concerned the effects of altitude. These effects range all the way from mild mental depression to death in violent spasms. Altitude and pressure changes affect us tremendously, and when it is realized that weather changes are similar to altitude changes, it follows that weather changes, too, certainly must affect us. True, a weather change might be slight by comparison in terms of barometric pressure, possibly the difference between sea level and a thousand feet or so above, but the further depressions of sunless sky and high humidity will all add up to quite a change in our mood. It is ridiculous to infer that all quarrels occur during high humidity or barometric depressions, but it is not ridiculous at all to state that such weather changes affect mental conditions and that quarrels do occur more often during such a period.

Moods can be changed by atmospheric changes and it wise to take this into consideration. The actions of drunken people are often overlooked and forgiven; but people can be drunk with humidity or heat, too. Many people even become extremely irritable in dry warmth;

it is well known that European trial courts frequently take heed of arguments that occur during the weather depression caused by the strange dry warmth of foehn winds. A murderer was once given a light sentence because he pleaded that his act was the result of emotions stirred by the foehn.

It is definitely established in medical and criminal reports that heat induces anger and that more crimes are committed during hot weather than in cold. It is not the heat alone that causes irritation, however, but either the dryness or the larger water content that the expanded warm air contains. In wise but plain words, *it ain't the heat, it's the humidity* that often irritates. The American Indians, who observed weather to a remarkable degree, knew well the effects of humidity upon man. "The Storm God gives courage to the Red Man," they said, and not a move during battle was made without a bit of weather-wise planning. Often battles were fought with the rain and wind to cover the attack. Actually, the high humidity and falling barometric pressure gave the Indians more irritability and more ability, therefore, to be warring fanatics.

During a time of warfare the Indian chief kept a scalp in his wigwam as a weather forecaster. Feeling the scalp for its limpness or liveliness, he could foretell the coming of rain just as many women today can by feeling their own hair. The most modern hygrometers, which measure humidity, still contain human hair, but science has found that blond hair is more reactive to humidity than brunette, so blond strands are used in these instruments.

There are people who insist that the financial market moves in rhythm with the barometer. There are wives who watch for the barometers to rise before asking their husbands for any special favor. But there is no point to definite rules of human behavior in relation to the weather, because we all respond differently to pressure changes. Although weather does affect us physically and mentally, we do not all generally react in the same way. To explain this statement, let me illustrate these pressure-change effects by telling you about the extreme pressure changes as encountered in aviation.

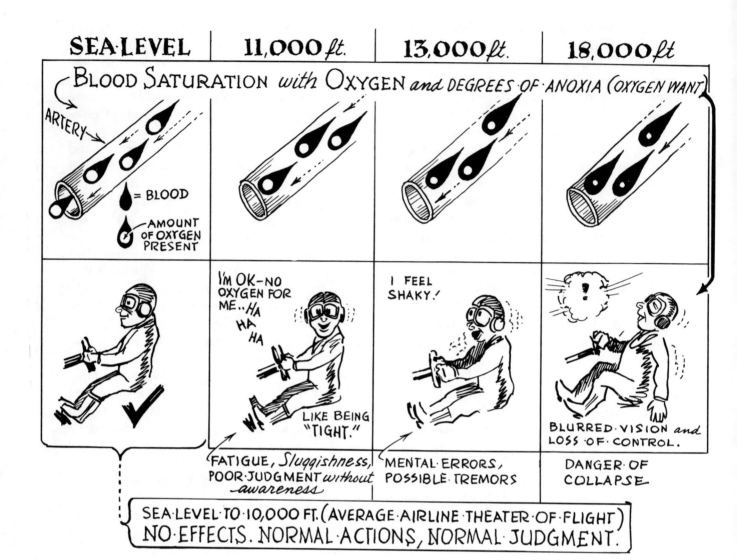

Drawing 5

Drawing 5 shows the effects of lowered pressure on an air pilot, along with a schematic diagram of the oxygen content of his bloodstream which causes that condition. Naturally, no weather change would equal the low air pressure of eleven thousand feet or more of altitude, but this exaggerated instance displays the important and instantaneous effect that pressure has upon the human body.

A study of Drawing 6 will acquaint the reader with the respiratory mechanics. Its simplified approach, designed for an Air Force manual, tells a quick story. One sees how pressure (the locomotive) is the important machine here — it pushes air in and enables the oxygen to be separated from it in the "lung refinery."

At this point it might be emphasized that, of all body necessities, oxygen is both the most important and the least stored. Man stores in his body energy and material of all kinds, but he has no storage place for even the smallest amount of oxygen. Therefore, the instant his oxygen supply is lowered or he is deprived of it he instantly experiences marked effects.

To illustrate this there is the story about a newly decorated dining room of a large hotel which strangely affected the people within it. The diners were too easily affected by drink and the entertainers too quickly exhausted by their performances. A weather-wise person sur-

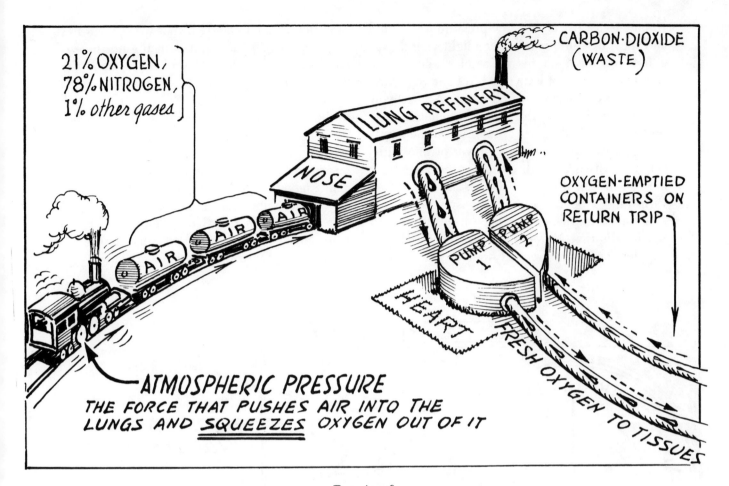

21% OXYGEN,
78% NITROGEN,
1% other gases

CARBON·DIOXIDE
(WASTE)

LUNG REFINERY

NOSE

OXYGEN-EMPTIED
CONTAINERS ON
RETURN TRIP

AIR   AIR   AIR

PUMP 1   PUMP 2

HEART

FRESH OXYGEN TO TISSUES

ATMOSPHERIC PRESSURE
THE FORCE THAT PUSHES AIR INTO THE
LUNGS AND SQUEEZES OXYGEN OUT OF IT

Drawing 6

mised that one of the room's attractions — the fact that it was entirely lit by candles — was causing these effects. Candles burn up oxygen quickly. They were removed and the situation was thus saved by a little air wisdom.

Although most people believe that high altitude is marked by a lack of oxygen, the oxygen proportion of upper air is practically the same; what differs mostly is density and pressure. It is the pressure of all the air above us that squeezes oxygen into our bloodstream to give us life; as soon as that pressure lowers, our life process slackens and anoxia (lack of oxygen) begins to take its course. No matter how a man dies, whether it be from disease, shock, drowning, or another cause, the actual and final reason for death will be anoxemia, failure of oxygen to reach the bloodstream fast enough. The most common display of anoxia occurs when the tissues are blocked

by alcohol so that pressure cannot squeeze oxygen into them. The drunken person may then react in many different ways: he may become belligerent, sad, extremely gay, or drowsy; his actions will be unsteady, his sight blurred, his memory poor. These very reactions are identical with those of the air pilot whose oxygen is lessened by the low pressure of high altitude: he will act in the exact same manner and do the same things he would do if he were intoxicated with liquor.

Not every time our faculties are impaired by a few stiff highballs do we have the same reactions. It follows also that the very mild physical reactions which occur with weather changes need not always be the same. The low pressure of pre-storm air sometimes makes one sad; at other times, drowsy, irritable, or gay; there is no set rule. But one is never so *alert* as during the high pressure of fine weather.

11

If one is aware of his low-pressure reactions and they are quite regular, he might well make a note of them on his barometer above the weather readings of FAIR and RAIN and STORMY, marking SAD, IRRITABLE, and so on. A salesman should be cautious during a barometric depression, and look to better sales when the hand swings upward; a depressed buyer or one with aching corns is a tough customer indeed. Trying to sell him during a "low" is as difficult as varnishing a boat in humid atmosphere.

A thousand years ago King Alfred observed, "So it falls that all men are with fine weather happier far." More recently our own weather-wise Ben Franklin advised that we "do business with men when the wind is in the northwest." He knew that when the wind is from that direction anywhere in the temperate zone of the Northern Hemisphere, the weather is likely to be buoyant, dry, and hopeful — the best state for quick decisions and for bold enterprises. So the barometer and wind-vane can be regarded as instruments for forecasting man's mood. Considering the old-timer's keen observation and the great variety of wind-vanes and barometers that have been designed, I am amazed that barometers such as the one suggested in Drawing 7 were never made.

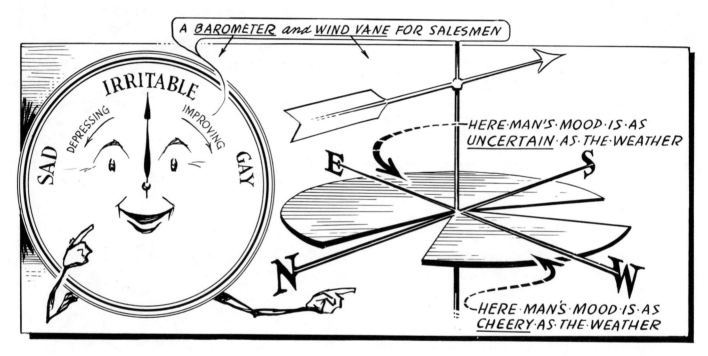

Drawing 7

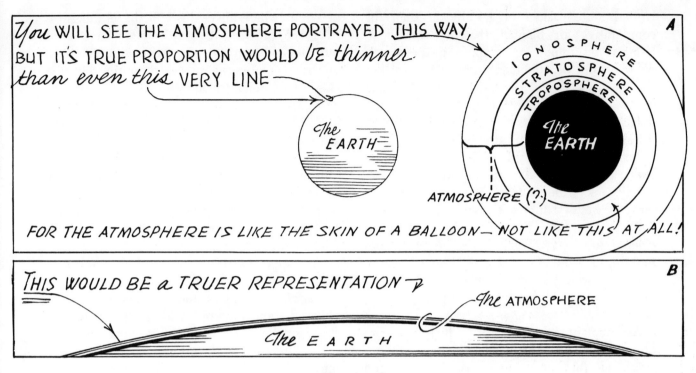

Drawing 8

2

THE ANATOMY OF AIR

To him who in the love of Nature holds
Communion with her visible forms, she speaks
A various language.

— BRYANT

A few years back we were all talking about being "air-minded." Of course what we really meant was aircraft-minded, or aviation-minded, because even the airplane pilot is not always air-minded or conscious of this stuff we live in and swim through. To be aware of air we must sort of feel and see it — something, I guess, that only the birds are really equipped to do. But we can try!

Before we begin to "see" air and to become aware of its anatomy we have a lot of textbook forgetting to do. For example, Drawing 8A above shows exactly how the meteorological books portray the earth and its blanket of atmosphere. Of course, this makes it look as

if the earth swims in a great sea of atmosphere which is divided into several layers. Nothing could be farther from the truth. To have shown the earth large enough for correct comparison with such a thickness of atmosphere, the printed page would have had to be twenty-five feet wide! Some books have tiny footnotes beneath such diagrams explaining the exaggeration, but a picture is so powerful that the damage of misinterpretation will have already occurred. Drawing 8B shows more correctly the thickness of the atmosphere as compared with the earth.

Actually the layer of atmosphere is so thin that a dime placed upon a large map of the

United States would be no thicker than the comparative air blanket that lies above it. Using a desk globe for comparison, the atmosphere would be about as thick as the varnish on its surface! No, the earth does not hang in a sea of air — it hangs in a sea of *space* and it has an extremely thin coating of gas on its surface. That gas is our atmosphere.

Actually the atmosphere is pretty squashy stuff. It's real, mind you, but squashy — like a haystack — the stuff at the bottom of the mass is wadded into a denser mass than the stuff at the top. For instance, if air were colored in tones of red, at the height of tall buildings it would be noticeably pink. At cloud height it would be pale and at stratospheric height one could hardly pick up any traces of red at all.

An airplane which lands at fifty miles an hour in New York City will find itself landing twice as fast at a high-altitude mountain airport where there is less air and therefore less air resistance. This is why airport landing strips must increase in length with the altitude of the airport, or, actually, with the thinness of the air. In the high Andes it is the custom of the natives to place heavy wet food out for the condors, then to hide and wait for the birds to feed. After the birds have fed, the hunters, leaping out from their nearby hiding place, can easily overtake the birds, which, with their added weight, must run farther through the thin atmosphere before flight is possible.

Bringing atmosphere down to earthly measurements seems strange to us, for we begin to measure something which we cannot see. Even the title "Anatomy of Air" sounds strange: air seems so much like a void. It is so much like a transparent, filmy nothingness; it can hardly seem to have any anatomy. Yet it has body and shape and density just like water or any part of the earth. *Part of the earth*, did I say? *That* is the important thing to remember, for air certainly is a part of the earth. Although we think of the surface of earth as being beneath our feet, the surface of the earth is really above our heads!

The surface of the earth is somewhere up above us where air ceases and the nothingness of space begins. It is this outer surface of our globe that makes our earth different from all other globes of space, primarily because this surface enables life to exist. We are not earth creatures as we are accustomed to think. We are all atmospheric beings. We can leave the ground, but not for a fraction of a second can we leave the atmosphere; only in atmosphere can living things exist. Our trouble in reaching other planets by rocket will not be so much in getting there as in learning how to take large enough chunks of earth's air along with us to exist.

The upper or stratospheric atmosphere cannot be explored by airplane because an airplane needs air to swim in and there is not enough of it up there to support flight, or enough for the propeller to bite into for propulsion. Of course, our so-called "gasoline engine" is really much more of an air engine; it uses many times more air than gasoline for its combustion mixture. Just as a candle would flicker and go out in a high altitude, an automobile engine would go slower and finally stop when it reached oxygen-poor heights. Jet planes also need much air; they fly by sucking air in front and shooting it out back. Balloons, however, can rise to extraordinary heights, well over a hundred thousand feet, but the lack of pressure at such altitudes soon causes the balloons to burst. Even the largest balloon, with only enough gas to lift its sagging folds upward, becomes as large as a ten-story apartment house at great heights, ready to burst itself into the low pressure of the thin stratosphere air. At 39,000 feet gas expands to seven times its sea-level size. I once prepared a chart to be hung in Air Force restaurants reminding fliers to go easy on soda-pop, hot dogs, beans, and other gassy foods because a blocked passage in their bodies at high altitude might mean extreme discomfort. I made cartoon balloons based upon the following gas-proportion data:

At 16,500 feet it is 2 times sea-level volume
At 25,000 feet it is 3 times sea-level volume
At 34,000 feet it is 5 times sea-level volume

Finding yourself with a parcel of gas trapped

inside you that has increased five times its size would be unbelievably painful. Just as our bodies are limited for expansion and lowering pressure, balloons are also limited. The biggest and most expansive balloon has reached only the lower parts of the stratosphere.

Upper-altitude exploration, then, depends upon the rocket, for it is a machine that does not need air for propulsion or buoyancy. It is even hindered by air! Space flight is fast because there is no air to slow one up. A ball thrown into space at twenty-five miles an hour would continue to roam the dark silent void of space throughout eternity at exactly twenty-five miles an hour. There would be nothing to slow it up and no reason for it to go faster, unless, as our meteors do, it encountered the gravitational force of a planet.

As soon as a weather student learns that the surface of the earth is above his head, he wants to know how far upward this atmospheric sea extends. Oddly enough, there is no answer, for air thins out gradually into nothingness. The thinning of air with altitude is so very gradual that there is no particular height where you can say, "Here air ends and space begins." The appreciable atmosphere, however, is said to extend for about twenty-five miles. By "appreciable" I don't mean "livable," I mean "measurable." The very sea-bottom of the atmosphere is the only truly appreciable part for us, because that is the only place where we find life. As Drawing 9 shows, about ten feet down in the solid earth and about three miles overhead, all known life ceases to be. We are confined to this comparatively thin film of our atmospheric deep sea.

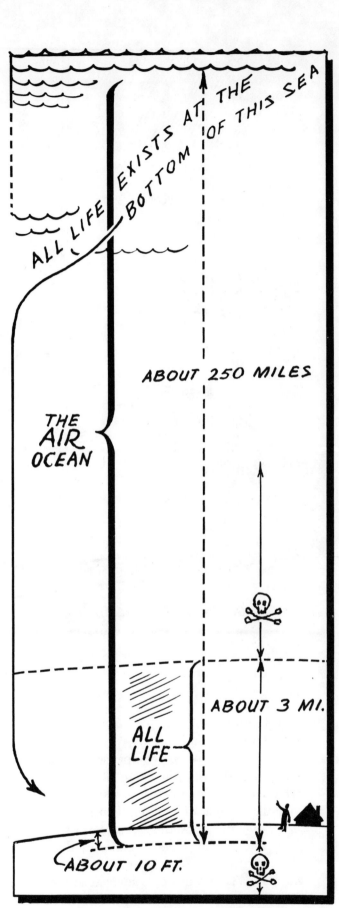

Drawing 9

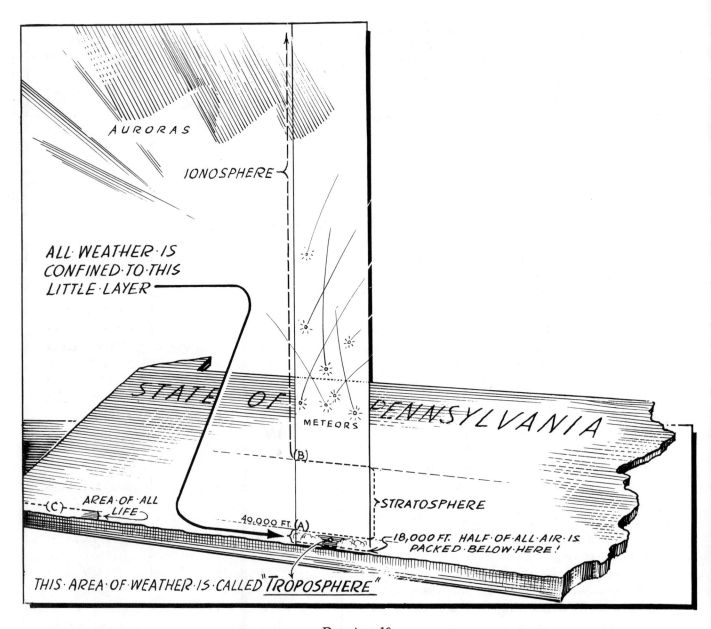

AURORAS

IONOSPHERE

ALL·WEATHER·IS
CONFINED·TO·THIS
LITTLE·LAYER

STATE·OF·PENNSYLVANIA

METEORS

(B)

AREA·OF·ALL
LIFE

(C)

40,000 FT. (A)

STRATOSPHERE

18,000 FT. HALF·OF·ALL·AIR·IS
PACKED·BELOW·HERE!

THIS·AREA·OF·WEATHER·IS·CALLED "TROPOSPHERE"

Drawing 10

It is pretty difficult to imagine what three miles upward and twenty-five miles upward are like. We need comparisons. Look at Drawing 10, with the state of Pennsylvania, which we can more or less visualize for size, and the comparative atmospheric heights that lie above it. Does this seem surprising?

In the drawing, line A indicates the top of the TROPOSPHERE (the layer where all weather occurs). That line, or TROPOPAUSE, is about 40,000 feet up. Above that, the STRATOSPHERE extends to an altitude of fifty miles, where the IONOSPHERE begins. The atmospheric molecules are so far apart in the ionosphere as to be practically immeasurable; yet they are present — as indicated by the auroral lights and by the reflecting layers that bounce radio waves back to us, making reception possible. The ionosphere is really the upper part of the stratosphere, where these ionized layers are. Possibly the word "ionosphere" will be dropped in time, and everything above the troposphere will just be called "stratosphere."

Notice, in the drawing, that at 18,000 feet

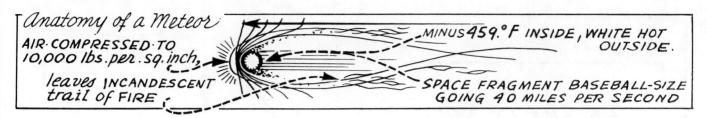

Drawing 11

half of all air is packed below and the other half fades away upward toward space. This is easily proved by taking a barometer (which measures the weight of air) to 18,000 feet; instead of its normal sea-level weight of about thirty inches of mercury, there will be just half of that or about 15 inches of mercury.

Not to depart from the subject of atmosphere, but to emphasize its existence all the more, Drawing 11 shows the anatomy of a meteor. The flaming flash of a "shooting star" is really not what one might think, for the speeding missile itself is not what lights up at all; it is the incandescence of the *air ahead of it* that could not get out of the way fast enough! The air ahead of so fast a thing gets packed into a white hot mass of compression; while the meteor itself may still maintain the coldness of space, the compressed air in front of it burns brightly. Many meteors that manage to reach the earth are found still cold, frosted, even freezing the ground around them, although their outside has been glazed by the heated air.

Before the meteoric mass enters the atmosphere its whole temperature is that of space, which is absolute zero, or −459°F. It may be attracted to the earth at about forty miles per second and slowed down to a "mere" ten thousand miles per hour when it strikes the thickness of atmosphere. This "slow collision" burns it up in a seventy-five-mile sweep of flame that we commonly call a "shooting star."

You may wonder how anything could be so cold on the inside yet be white-hot on the outside. But if you imagine putting a blowtorch to a cake of ice you will realize that the inside of the cake could maintain its normal temperature while the outside melted away. The two cases are quite similar.

We can be compared to submarine animals on the bottom of the sea and meteors to missiles shot down toward us; these missiles never reach us because the surface "water" slows them up and disintegrates them before they can strike the bottom of the atmospheric sea. The moon, which has no atmospheric sea around it, is bombarded constantly by billions of meteors.

Although the air up above us is very, very thin, it is still thick enough to interfere with meteoric space travelers and to introduce them to earth with a flaming halt. Certainly if meteors had mentality, they would be very much aware that the upper atmosphere is really the surface of the earth, for very few of them manage to hurtle down through this outer earthly layer.

When you look at the moon you can see its surface clearly because the moon has no atmosphere enveloping it. If you were on the moon, looking back at the earth, you could not even see our continents; the earth would be one bright fluid-looking "moon" because of its atmosphere blanket. Living things do not exist on the moon because of its atmosphere-lack. If you could encase yourself in a suit of air-and-pressure to keep you alive there, you would find all sorts of queer things happening because of the absence of air. There would be no sound (sound travels by air) and there would be only intense sun-heat or cold shadow (air filters sunlight), so that you would either burn or freeze. Of course you would be constantly bombarded by space fragments.

17

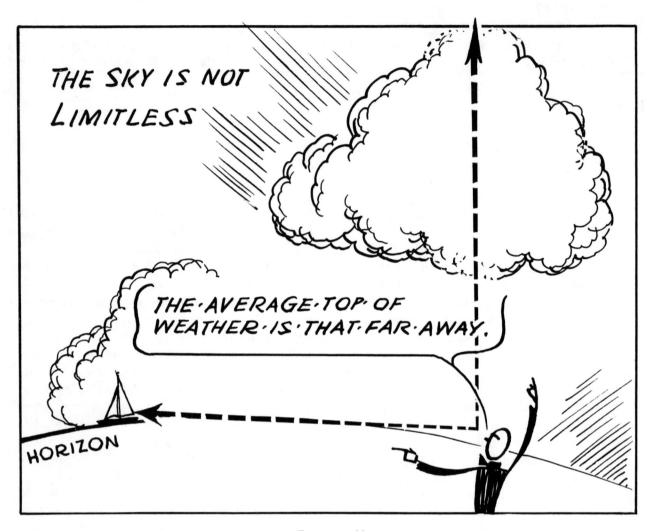

Drawing 12

And now back to the earth and its air and weather. After disappointing the student by not being able to give a definite height to atmosphere, let's try to answer his next question: "How high is *weather?*" Drawing 12 gives a fair visual answer; the average weather confine is no farther above you than the horizon is away from you, which makes the "sky" seem pretty close. Drawing 13 gives a better picture, showing that clouds and weather occur only where heat and humidity (the ingredients of weather) abound close to the warm, wet ground. This area of mixing atmosphere extends to an average of seven and a half miles and is called the troposphere. Within the troposphere, all cloudform and

18

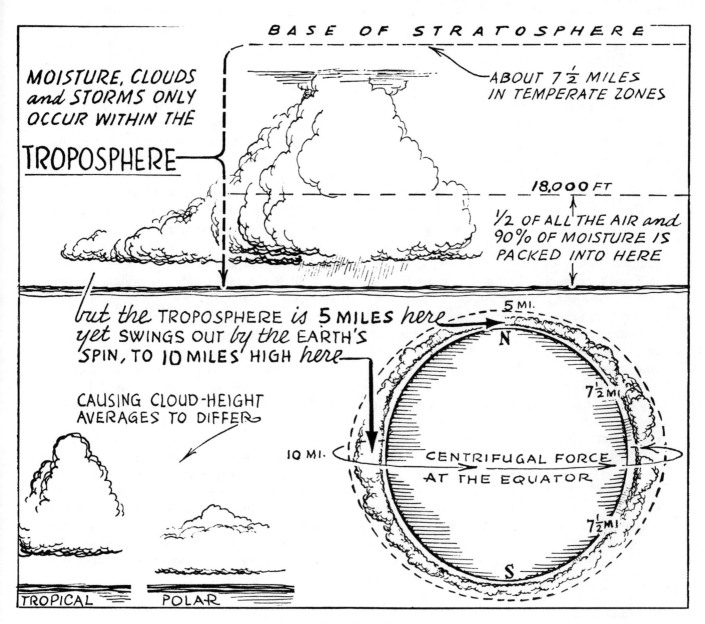

Drawing 13

precipitation occur. The second part of Drawing 13 explains why the troposphere (clouds and all) is higher at the equator than at the poles. Of course everyone knows that the earth is not exactly round, that it is swung out into a bulge at the middle by centrifugal force. Well, so is the atmosphere, but to a greater degree, for the difference in height is about five miles. This is why one heard of wartime pilots encountering thunderheads that towered to fifty thousand feet, even higher than bombers could reach; they were just flying in the "bulged-out atmosphere" of the tropics. It follows that one can expect to find the clouds of middle latitudes at medium heights and the clouds at the poles very low.

3

AIR HAS WEIGHT

When air gets light,
The glass falls low,
Batten down tight,
For the winds will blow.
— OLD SEA CHANTEY

A fish cannot be aware of water pouring from one place to another. He lives within the element; he can't even see it. We cannot picture our air flowing, either; but if air were poured out from a big pitcher in space, it would flow by its own weight, exactly like water, envelop the earth, and seek its own level.

The fact that cooled air shrinks, or packs denser and becomes heavier, is one of the secrets of weather lore. The changes in weight (caused mainly by heat differences) cause air to flow this way and that, and new weather to evolve. One can see in Drawing 14 how sun-warmed atmosphere will set up a machinery of motion that results in the simplest form of wind, the daytime sea breeze and the night land breeze. The land during the day is like a warm stove with most of the air rising chimney-fashion; it is natural that some air should rush in from the sea to take the place of the rising atmosphere; thus, presto, a sea breeze!

Another important feature in the winds that go up and down derives from their wetness. One would certainly think that wet air would be heavier; but no, dry air is heavier! This fact aids evaporation, cloud formation, and many other weather phenomena; it also explains why moist air is carried up where clouds begin.

But no matter how many times we say that "air has weight," it's just too difficult a picture to visualize at once. For instance, it is difficult to realize that a broken electric light bulb weighs more than an unbroken one which, of course, with its partial vacuum, contains less air. Or you cannot visualize the air from your room if it were packed into suitcase size; it would be so heavy that few men could lift it! A space-ship engineer was discussing the effect of gravity on air. "Beyond gravitation," he said, "we'd run into all sorts of strange problems. When we breathed outward our breath would not rise as warm air should. It would stay smack in front of us and we'd be breathing the same air back again every time."

We are atmospheric creatures who depend upon high air pressure for life. We don't find uncomfortable the normal sea-level weight of air, which is about fifteen pounds per square inch. But add that up to the total of the fourteen tons or so that press against your outside surface, and the thought begins to seem incredible. Once I flew to a very high altitude on an oxygen experiment, wearing a nice new waterproof (airtight) watch. When the outside air became thin and of low pressure, the tiny bit of high pressure inside my watch actually blew the crystal off!

One of the reasons that we find it hard to visualize air having weight is because atmospheric weight is always referred to as pressure. (The weight of a gas *presses* out in all directions.) The pressure of air is caused by the weight of all the air above that presses down on whatever air there is below.

Drawing 15 compares air with water to show how this pressure down near the earth is greater than the pressure up and away from it. A big tank of water will simply drip from a leak located near the top, while it will squirt with great pressure if the leak is at the bottom. Air and water, which are both fluids (flowing material), act very much alike, so we shall use this comparison often.

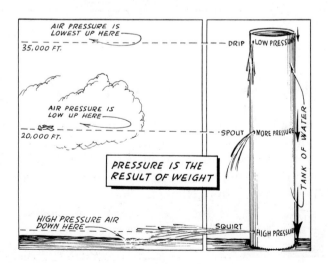

AIR PRESSURE IS
LOWEST UP HERE
35,000 FT.

AIR PRESSURE IS
LOW UP HERE
20,000 FT.

PRESSURE IS THE
RESULT OF WEIGHT

HIGH PRESSURE AIR
DOWN HERE

DRIP LOW PRESSURE

SPOUT MORE PRESSURE

TANK OF WATER

SQUIRT HIGH PRESSURE

20

Drawing 15

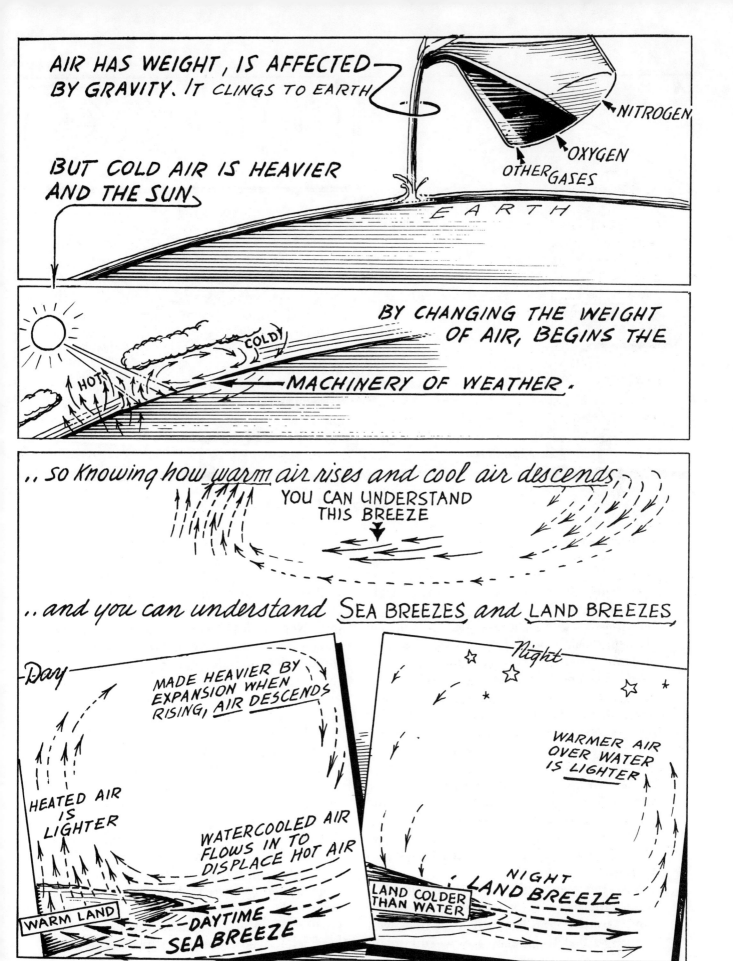

Drawing 14

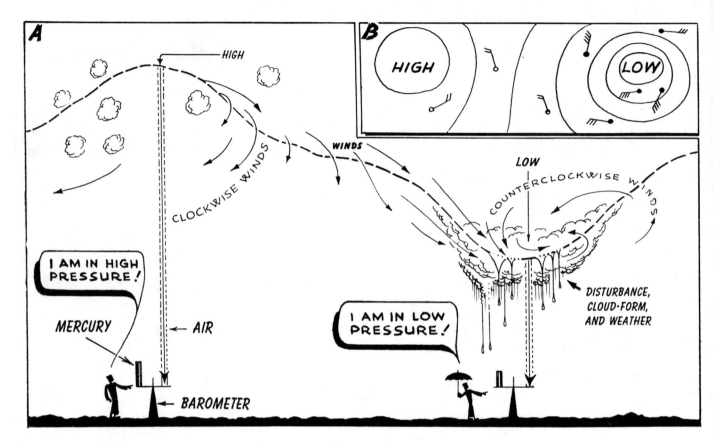

Drawing 16

Drawing 16 shows Chicago with a "high-pressure atmosphere" and New York with a "low-pressure atmosphere." The pressure in Chicago is high because there is a mountain of density overhead pressing down on it; New York's pressure is low because there is a valley of density overhead with less weight pressing down there. Notice the column of air that presses down on each city's barometer. Notice, too, how the air (again like water) flows *off* the mountain and *into* the valley. Why they flow clockwise and counterclockwise, we shall take up later. Now look at Drawing 16B and see how the same picture would be seen from overhead in a weather-map form. Here our comparison of weights has become a comparison of pressures — high and low.

Now the picture shown in Drawing 16 is not a stationary one, for this whole air contour moves, usually from left to right or from west to east, so that the low over New York might

well pass out over the Atlantic and the high over Chicago would then be expected to pass over New York. One can imagine how these changes in air pressure would be forecast largely through locating the positions and routes of the roaming atmospheric mountains and valleys above us. We cannot see them to locate them, but we can weigh all the air above and be on the watch for changes of weight. This brings us to the barometer, which is our air-weighing machine.

Very much like our Chicago and New York drawing, but with the high and low reversed for variety, Drawing 17 shows the barometer principle enlarged. Always, the column of mercury acts as a balance-weight against a like column of all the air above. Naturally, the more air density there is above, the more height and weight of mercury is needed to balance that greater air weight. So there you have it: the barometer is no more than a plain scales that

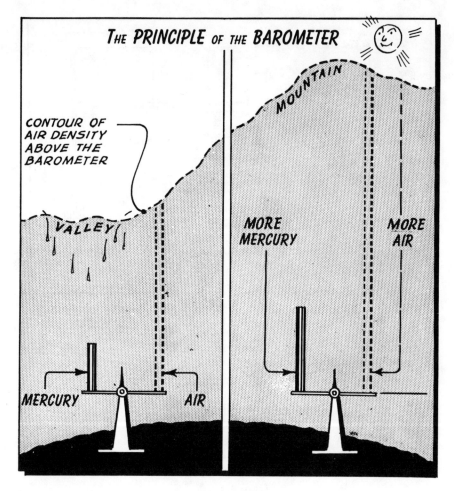

CONTOUR OF AIR DENSITY ABOVE THE BAROMETER

MOUNTAIN

VALLEY

MORE MERCURY

MORE AIR

MERCURY

AIR

Drawing 17

weighs the mountains and valleys of air that pass overhead. When the barometer is high, it reveals that a mountain of good-weather density is pressing its weight down on us and all the surrounding atmosphere is flowing downhill toward some outlying rainy low-pressure area.

Here is something important to remember: the actual reading on a barometer is often very little indication of anything. The thing one really wants to know is if the barometer is rising, falling, steady, or unsteady. In this way one can tell whether the present outside weather is liable to change and, if so, whether for better or worse.

The first barometer used water as a balance-weight. But to equal the weight of a like-sized tube of atmosphere overhead, the barometric tube of water had to be over thirty feet long. This did not make for a very portable or

convenient air-weighing machine. And besides, water evaporates. So a nonevaporable and much heavier fluid had to be found; of course, mercury was the answer. Mercury has now become the standard air-weighing counterweight. We now say the pressure in New York is so many "inches," which refers to the length of a tube of mercury that counterbalances the weight of all the air over New York in a like-sized tube. The average sea-level height of mercury in a barometer is between 29 and 30 inches.

You can understand how, if you carried a barometer to a greater height, it would have less air above it and, as a result, its mercury balance-weight would go down. Accepting *that*, you can see how every barometer can be an altimeter, too. In fact, the aviators' altimeter is just an ANEROID BAROMETER. Don't let the word "aneroid" confuse you; an aneroid barometer

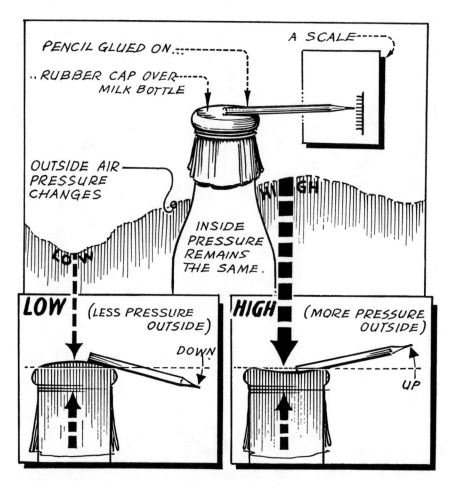

PENCIL GLUED ON

A SCALE

RUBBER CAP OVER MILK BOTTLE

OUTSIDE AIR PRESSURE CHANGES

INSIDE PRESSURE REMAINS THE SAME.

HIGH

LOW

LOW (LESS PRESSURE OUTSIDE)

DOWN

HIGH (MORE PRESSURE OUTSIDE)

UP

Drawing 18

is simply one that does not use fluid. Instead, it imprisons average-pressure air within a metal box; when the outside air changes, the box's lid presses inward or outward and that in turn actuates a dial.

My grocer has a lot of aneroid barometers on his shelf, in the form of coffee sealed in "vacuum-packed" cans. Of course, the vacuum is not a complete one, but the pressure inside the can is simply less than the pressure outside; when you open the can you can hear the outside atmosphere rush in with a *pfuff* sound. Although the outside atmosphere changes with weather differences, the trapped air of the coffee can remains the same, so that very often its lid will move up and down before bad weather, making ghostly popping noises. You have probably often opened a bottle partially filled with liquid and heard a slight inrush or outrush of air: this sound indicated that the

pressure and the weather were quite different when last you closed the cap.

The aneroid principle is shown in a method I devised, which I am sure the Weather Bureau will not use. But you can experiment with it and all you need is a pencil, a piece of sheet rubber, and a milk bottle. I refer you to Drawing 18. As soon as you cover the bottle with the rubber, remember that you are imprisoning the air pressure of that very moment. If tomorrow's or the next hour's outside atmosphere changes its pressure, you will know it by seeing the way the rubber bulges inward or outward. Of course, you must not put your bottle barometer in the sun, for then the air inside will heat and expand; then you'd have a complicated thermometer-barometer, or something. Leave it in the shade and you will be interested to watch it move with the atmospheric changes.

24

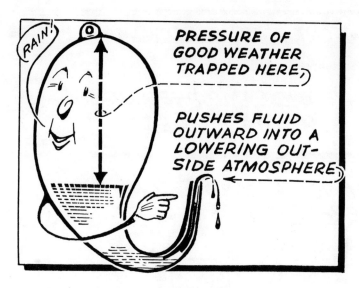

Drawing 19

We cannot conclude a discussion of barometers without mentioning the Cape Cod weather-indicator. Drawing 19 shows how it works. One imprisons some "air of the day" within, by shutting it off with some colored water. When the outside air changes its pressure, the colored water, which is now between two pressures, either rises or falls.

Barometers are delicate things and difficult to use for weather prediction unless they are used along with other information. For example, if one uses the barometer with wind-direction information, one has a fair prophecy. A chart of this nature should be kept alongside the barometer to make it more valuable throughout the United States:

WIND DIRECTION	PRESSURE	WEATHER
E to N	Low, falling fast	Severe gale, rain
E to N	Low but rising	Cold wave
S to E	Falling	Storm, clearing in 24 hours
S to SW	Rising	Clear soon, several good days ahead
SE to NE	Falling	Rain for 1 or 2 days
E to NE	Falling	Rain in 24 hours
S to SE	Falling	Wind, rain in 18 hours
SW to NW	Steady	Fair for 2 days
SW to NW	Rising fast	Fair, rain in 2 days
Going to West	Rising	Clearing, colder

The diurnal or daily effect is one that few barometer readers take into consideration. Temperature brings noticeable pressure differences. The heat of day thins out the atmosphere while the cold of night makes it dense and heavy. This effect can be read on the barograph and should be taken into consideration when making barometric readings. The diurnal variation is an atmospheric tide which is fairly strong in southern latitudes but vanishes in latitudes above sixty degrees. The daily pressure tends to be highest at 10 A.M. and 10 P.M., lowest at 4 A.M. and 4 P.M. The amount of change is only about .04 inches in the middle latitudes and about .15 in the tropics. The significance of this is that a slight falling of the barometer does not necessarily forebode a change in the weather, but may be due to diurnal variation.

25

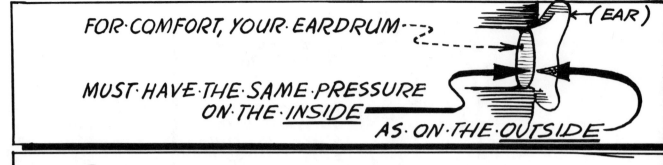

FOR·COMFORT, YOUR·EARDRUM·--→ (EAR)

MUST·HAVE·THE·SAME·PRESSURE ON·THE·INSIDE

AS·ON·THE·OUTSIDE

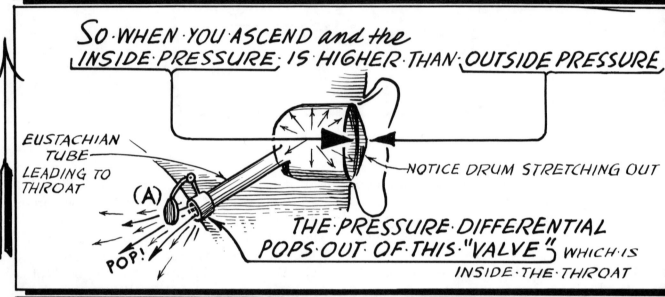

SO·WHEN·YOU·ASCEND and the INSIDE·PRESSURE·IS·HIGHER·THAN·OUTSIDE PRESSURE

EUSTACHIAN TUBE LEADING TO THROAT

(A)

NOTICE DRUM STRETCHING OUT

POP!

THE·PRESSURE·DIFFERENTIAL POPS·OUT·OF·THIS·"VALVE" WHICH·IS INSIDE·THE·THROAT

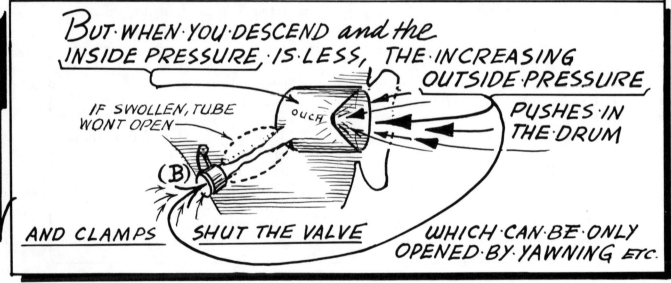

BUT·WHEN·YOU·DESCEND and the INSIDE PRESSURE·IS·LESS, THE·INCREASING OUTSIDE·PRESSURE

IF SWOLLEN, TUBE WONT OPEN

OUCH

PUSHES·IN THE·DRUM

(B)

AND CLAMPS SHUT THE VALVE WHICH·CAN·BE·ONLY OPENED·BY·YAWNING ETC.

Drawing 20

We have discussed the weight of air, how we weigh it, and how we make weather maps and predict weather changes with this information. But have you ever noticed the difference that air weights have upon *you?* Inside of us we have many cavities that are (or become) occasionally blocked off; when the outside air weight changes, we still have the unchanged air pressure inside. And *ouch!* There are the sinuses and the inner ear, for example. When the weather and pressure change, the sinuses begin to "act up." Go to the doctor and he "opens them up," so that your outside pressure may equal your inside pressure, the air flowing in and out with every change.

You have probably noticed that the airline stewardess will offer you a piece of gum to chew just before the plane descends to land. Drawing 20 explains why. Your eardrum is a thin skin stretched like a door across the hallway of the inner-ear cavity. As soon as the pressure on one side of the "rubber door" becomes greater than the pressure on the other, the door bulges under the strain. Bulge it too far and you will get a broken door (a broken or ruptured eardrum). Look at Drawing 20 (A) which makes the eardrum seem exactly like the rubber cover over our "aneroid barometer" milk bottle.

Fortunately nature has put in a safety valve called the EUSTACHIAN TUBE, which lets the differential in pressure in or out, as the case may be. You open this tube every time you swallow and every time you yawn; you can tell because it makes a tiny click in your ears when you do it. Try it now and see. The valve (20A and B) is back in the throat near each ear.

Nature, however, did not foresee our very rapid descents in elevators or in airplanes, for she designed the Eustachian tube so that, although high pressure air can blow out of the valve as shown at (A), air cannot blow itself back into the tube — look at (B). So you must open it yourself, either by yawning, swallowing, or yelling; chewing a stick of gum is the simplest way to keep opening your Eustachian tube.

The drawing (B), however, shows a blocked tube, which occurs when you have a cold or other ear infection. This sketch was done for the Air Force and its message told fighter pilots not to fly when they had bad colds.

Sudden weather or pressure changes may affect your sinuses and inner cavities. And they may explain that urge to yawn when a skyscraper elevator, or a train rushing into an under-river tunnel, gives you an odd uncomfortable sensation in your ears. Nature has made the yawn contagious so that, even though we might forget to do so now and then, we can hardly watch another person do it without following suit.

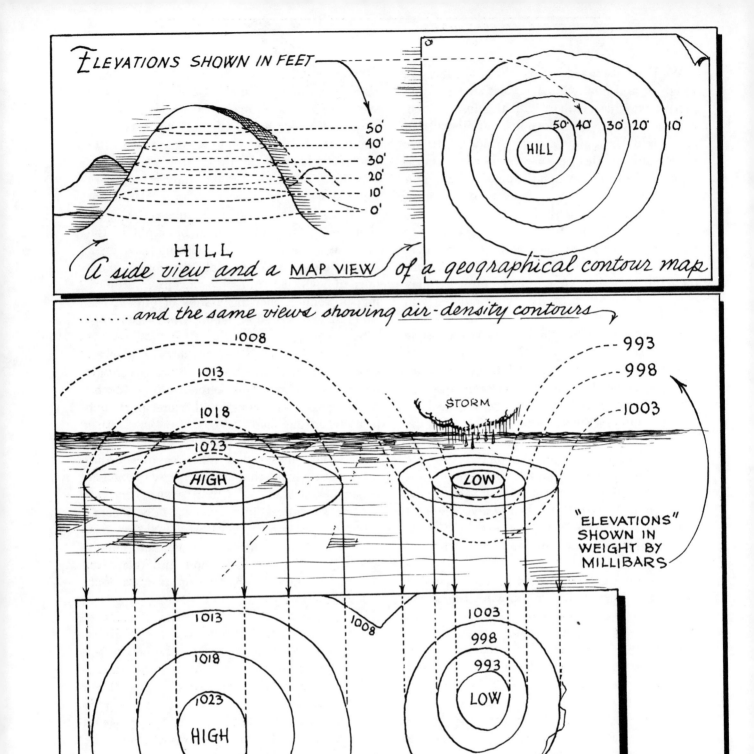

ELEVATIONS SHOWN IN FEET

50'
40'
30'
20'
10'
0'

HILL

50' 40' 30' 20' 10'

HILL

A side view and a MAP VIEW of a geographical contour map

.......and the same views showing air-density contours

1008
1013
1018
1023

993
998
1003

STORM

HIGH

LOW

"ELEVATIONS"
SHOWN IN
WEIGHT BY
MILLIBARS

1013
1018
1023

1008

1003
998
993

HIGH

LOW

1008

ISOBAR

WEATHER MAP

Drawing 21

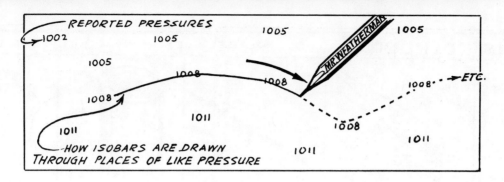

REPORTED PRESSURES

1002   1005   1005   1005

1005

1008   1008   MR WEATHERMAN   1008 → ETC.

1008

1011   1008

1011   1008

HOW ISOBARS ARE DRAWN
THROUGH PLACES OF LIKE PRESSURE   1011   1011

Drawing 21A

4

ISOBARS

*Science is the topography
of ignorance.*

— HOLMES

This will be a brief chapter with very few words but enough picture material to take the place of a great many words.

The business of weighing the atmosphere is the basis for making all weather maps. As shown above in Drawing 21A, if you draw a line through numbers representing the cities where the air pressures are identical, you will be automatically drawing an ISOBAR, just as a weather-map maker does it. Iso means "like" and BAR refers to "barometric pressure," so an isobar would be a line of equal or like barometric pressure drawn across a map.

Now, because we are all familiar with geographical contour maps, Drawing 21 which compares the geographical contour map (above) with a weather contour map (below), is very helpful and self-explanatory. When next you look at a weather map, begin your analysis by first getting the picture of its atmospheric contours—just as if you were looking at a land map instead of an air map. You will then begin to really *see* the air picture of its contours.

The measurements on weather-map isobars were once shown only by numbers which indicated the height of the mercury column, but since aneroid barometers have been perfected,

another measurement has come to be used, called MILLIBARS. Exactly what a millibar is, is beside the point. It would make no difference if we measured air by the weight of apples or oysters. The point is that air pressure is higher or lower at one place than it is at another, or if it is going up or coming down. However, most weather maps put inches-of-mercury measurements on one end of each isobar and millibars on the other end; you can take your choice. The purpose is simply to visualize the action of the contours of air density and to encircle all highs and lows with isobaric boundary lines.

In general you will find that the isobars encircling a high are farther apart than those around a low, which indicates that lows have steeper gradients and higher winds, which of course is to be expected in stormy areas. Drawing 21B gives an elementary conception of this difference between close isobars and distant isobars. Air, which rushes from high pressure to low pressure, can be seen rushing exactly like water which goes from high altitude to low altitude. The flags demonstrate that the area of close isobars has the most wind, while the area of distant isobars has the most calm.

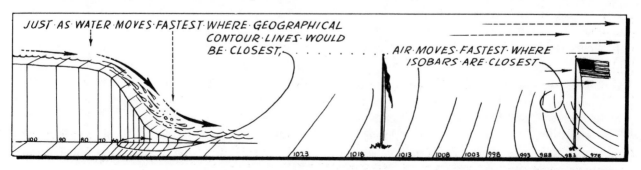

JUST AS WATER MOVES FASTEST WHERE GEOGRAPHICAL
CONTOUR LINES WOULD
BE CLOSEST, ...   AIR MOVES FASTEST WHERE
ISOBARS ARE CLOSEST

100 90 80 70 60   1023 1018 1013 1008 1003 998 993 988 983 978

Drawing 21B

THIS IS FOLKLORE — DO YOU BELIEVE THEM? COULD SOME BE TRUE?

VINES? CLIMB TO THE RIGHT

WHIRLPOOLS? TEND TO SWIRL RIGHTWISE

TRAINS? WEAR THEIR RIGHT WHEELS FIRST.

TREES? GRAIN TENDS TO LEAN TO RIGHT.

WATER? EMPTIES MOSTLY TO THE RIGHT

THIS IS SO — — THESE THINGS VEER RIGHT-WISE *in the* NORTHERN HEMISPHERE.

HIGH BANK   LOW BANK
RIVERS
RIVERS CUT INTO THE RIGHT BANK

PROJECTILES
VEER IN FLIGHT GOING RIGHTWISE

WEATHER
ALL WINDS VEER TO THEIR RIGHT

OCEAN CURRENTS
ALL OCEAN CURRENTS SWIRL TO THE RIGHT

HURRICANES
ARE CORIOLIS MECHANISMS

Drawing 22

5   WEATHER IS A CIRCULAR AFFAIR

Heavenly clouds who supply us with thought and argument and intelligence and humbug and circumlocution, and ability to hoax, and comprehension.
— ARISTOPHANES

After explaining that wind is simply air rushing from high pressure to low pressure, it is difficult to explain why on the weather maps it may be seen rushing not so much from the highs to the lows as *around* them. At earth levels, wind moves from the high to the low pressure, simply enough, and the wind arrows may be seen crossing isobars at about 45 degrees. But beginning at a relatively low altitude, the wind flows *with* the isobars, clockwise around the highs and counterclockwise around the lows. This strange arrangement reverses itself in the Southern Hemisphere. The scientific law says that all free, large-scale movements in the Northern Hemisphere veer

to the right; they veer to the left in the Southern Hemisphere. One asks why this happens, and also what "the law" is.

It is all caused by something called EARTH DEFLECTIVE FORCE, CORIOLIS FORCE, or FERREL'S LAW; it can be explained and proved by equations — which, unfortunately, only a student of mathematics can readily understand. If the scientists will excuse my pictorial diagrams and sensationalism, look to the folklore drawings at the top of Drawing 22, then to the truths at the bottom. They both deal with this strange deflective force.

There are hundreds of odd folk sayings about the "force" first given the name of Coriolis.

30

As a result of this force, it is said, drunks fall, snakes coil, dogs make their beds, and sea shells curl, all according to the law, all doing it clockwise in one hemisphere and counterclockwise in the other. One can experiment with it by emptying the water in wash basins or swimming pools with maddening results. What are the facts behind the folklore?

About a hundred years ago a scientist, William Ferrel, stated: "In whatever direction a body moves on the surface of the earth, there is a force arising from the earth's rotation which deflects it to the right in the Northern Hemisphere and to the left in the Southern." This effect is called an illusion and a non-absolute force because it is really we ourselves and the earth that do the deflecting, *not* the moving body. Nevertheless, one half of our globe is full of things dervishing to the right, while the opposite side finds the same things going the other way.

For instance, if a big gun is fired in the middle northern latitudes, during the three miles and twelve seconds of its flight the bullet will have veered ten feet to the right. Actually the projectile went straight (according to Newton's Law), but, as the earth turned beneath, its course was a mathematically true arc. In the Southern Hemisphere the veering would have been to the left. It is also perfectly true that rivers, as they flow to the sea, veer to the right (in the Northern Hemisphere), causing their right banks to be steep and their left banks to be more gradual, particularly in the middle latitudes.

Oceans are controlled by this strange force, gyrating according to the hemisphere in which they are located, as may be seen by the arrows on any global map featuring ocean currents. The whole North Atlantic, for instance, has a very definite gyration from left to right, making a complete circle in about three years. Weather is controlled by Coriolis, with winds veering to the right and making complete aerial whirlpools. A hurricane, for instance, is a Coriolis machine twisting counterclockwise in the Northern Hemisphere.

Scientific papers were written about deflection effects as far back as 1775; for instance, Laplace on air and ocean tides. The existence of an effect on artillery fire was explicitly realized during the Civil War, although imperfect equipment then in use could make no correction for it.

Let us now see why this strange controlling force is called an illusion. Imagine yourself at the North Pole throwing a ball to a man on the equator, as shown in Drawing 23. Of course, the ball actually will go straight, but the man on the equator will have moved with the rotating earth. A camera would show the ball making a curve and falling far to the right of its mark. If you threw the ball from the South Pole, it would have veered to the left.

But this confuses all weather students, who

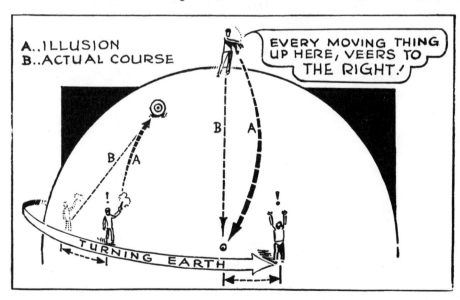

Drawing 23

know that, although movements veer to the *right* low-pressure areas move counterclockwise, which is definitely to the *left*. Why should highs and lows, both controlled by Coriolis, move oppositely? Drawing 24 shows why in a way that you will never forget. A high is a mountain of air density, while a low is a sinkhole. Ordinarily anything would flow directly off a mountain, and directly into a sinkhole. But like the little man on a sled that veers to the right, winds flowing off a high will spiral completely around, clockwise. The opposite is true of a sinkhole. Study this

drawing carefully; it is the first of its kind and should make your weather-map reading simpler. "Low" winds flow inside a "sinkhole" while "high" winds flow down the sides of a "hill."

Because winds circle counterclockwise around a low, one may face the wind, and point to his right at the nearest low (storm area). Try this and check the findings on a weather map. If the low is to the west, then, traveling at a rate of about five hundred miles a day, it should reach you.

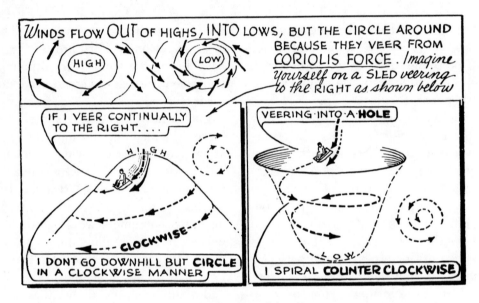

Drawing 24

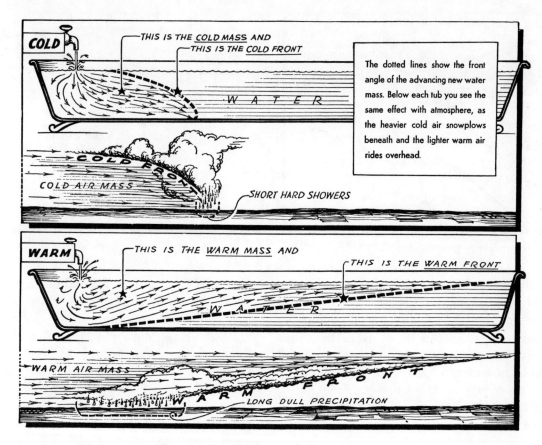

Drawing 25

6

FRONTS AND MASSES

Knowledge alone is the being of Nature,
Giving a soul to her manifold features.
— BAYARD TAYLOR

Step by step we are coming to the subject of understanding the weather map. A few years ago the weather map consisted only of isobars and shaded areas that showed where it was raining. Today we have FRONTS. Cold ones, warm ones, stationary ones, and occluded ones. And, although we are all familiar with the map's fencelike front-symbols, few of us really know what a front or its mechanism looks like.

Drawing 25 gives another elementary sketch that compares air with water. I once made glass containers like the tubs shown, and used colored cold water in one instance, then colored hot water in the next; so I know they act as shown. When cold water comes out of the faucet, the new mass advances like a snowplow with a downward-sloping front; atmosphere acts

in the same way, as shown in the sketch below the tub. Next, you see warm water coming out of the faucet, leaning this time with a forward-sloping front; again you may see in the sketch below that air acts in the same way. In both cases, a FRONT is simply the front wall of an advancing MASS of differently temperatured stuff. If it will either amuse or educate you, the next time you find yourself standing in a tub of room-temperature water, turn on the cold water and then the hot. The cold water will creep down and attack your toes first, while the hot water will rise and attack you at the waterline level. Of course, you must stand away from the faucets; don't feel too silly about it — you are being a scientist in the bathtub!

33

Drawing 26

At this point let me emphasize the fact that a cold front does not have to be very cold or a warm front to be very warm. A summer cold front could consist of air at 79°F., which is pretty warm to the average person. But it would be considered "cold" if it were advancing on hot air of 100°F. What makes a front "cold" or "warm" is only the fact that it is colder or warmer than the air it displaces.

Looking back at the drawing of fronts, it is easy to see their differences. The cold wall slants backward, whereas the warm wall slants overhead in a forward manner. The cold front leaves clear, dry, cold air in its wake while the warm front leaves warm, wet air behind. The fast, steeper, cold front causes shorter but harder rains, while the delicately slanted and slower warm front features longer, slower rains. The cold front covers a hundred miles or less, while the warm front covers a probable eight hundred miles or more.

Weather students will very often look at an approaching storm to try to see the actual frontal angle. Forget it. On rare occasions, in an airplane, one can see a concentrated cold-front slant, but from the ground this is hardly possible. And if you think you could see a warm-front slant, remember that the slant is 1 to 200. If the warm-front diagram were to be correctly portrayed and if it were one inch high, the page would have to be over twenty feet wide. An automobile would not even roll on such a slight slant. For example, if the prow of a warm front is sliding over New York its rainy tail is probably dragging Chicago.

Of course, the weather map is a surface

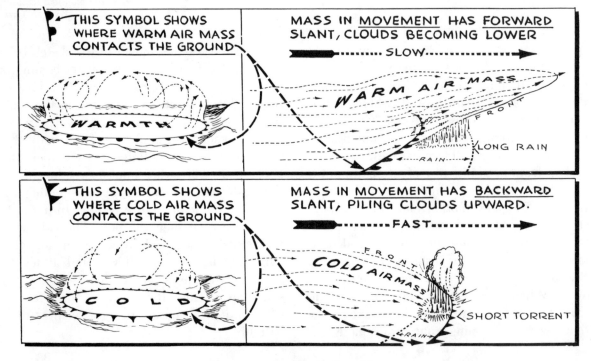

Drawing 27

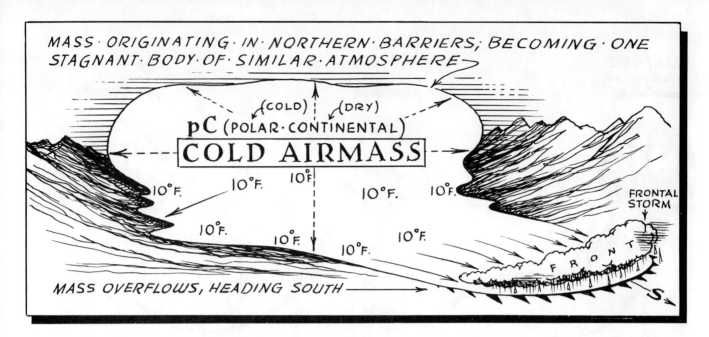

MASS·ORIGINATING·IN·NORTHERN·BARRIERS; BECOMING·ONE STAGNANT·BODY·OF·SIMILAR·ATMOSPHERE

(COLD)   (DRY)
pC (POLAR·CONTINENTAL)
COLD AIRMASS

10°F.   10°F.   10°F   10°F.   10°F.

10°F.   10°F.   10°F.   10°F.

FRONTAL STORM

FRONT

S

MASS OVERFLOWS, HEADING SOUTH

Drawing 28

affair, and therefore shows a frontal symbol where the slanting front actually comes in contact with the earth. You can see how the warm-front symbol would move far ahead in weather maps at 5000 feet, 10,000 feet, 20,000 feet, and so on.

Why should anyone want to know where the fronts are? And why didn't the weather maps always have fronts on them? That is a simple and basic story. Most people used to think that if today happened to be warmer, it was simply yesterday's air with heat added. Or if today were colder, it was yesterday's air with some heat lost. Sounds logical, doesn't it? But no; weather is a *moving* thing. Masses of warmer and colder air go roaming around the country, bumping into each other and generally causing the atmospheric confusion that results in rain and all other weather changes. The air you are now breathing was probably five hundred miles to the west yesterday; and the air you exhale at this moment will be just as far off tomorrow!

Like the foam and fuss that gather at the prow of a moving ship, clouds and rain most frequently gather at the front wall or along the front of an advancing AIR MASS. Therefore if your weather map plots the position and course of new air masses by marking down their fronts, you can expect this or that sort of weather with a great deal more certainty. That is why the map maker enjoys finding fronts

— he is being a weather detective and plotting weather changes for you. Drawing 26 shows a cold front and a warm front as seen from the side, then as seen from above or on a weather map, showing the two map symbols used — triangles for cold and semicircles for warm, both placed in direction of movement.

You can hardly mention fronts without first mentioning what they are the front *of*. Fronts of things don't go roaming about without the things themselves, do they? In Hollywood studios, perhaps, but not in nature. So we come to the air masses, or things behind the fronts. Drawings 27 and 28 give an idea of what goes on behind the fronts. Both pictures tell almost the same story, but remember these sketches are not mathematical diagrams so much as fluid pictures to impress upon you the anatomy of air. So overlook the repetition and do study both of them.

A few years ago there was no such thing in meteorology as an air mass; today weather maps are overladen with a tangle of fronts indicating the boundaries of air masses that come and go, causing weather changes. Most sailors are familiar with the various fronts and the storms that accompany them, but few are familiar with the masses behind the fronts. A cold front, for example, is a comparatively narrow strip of weather, while the actual cold mass itself may last for days and will be of the greatest importance. It is my prediction that popular weather

35

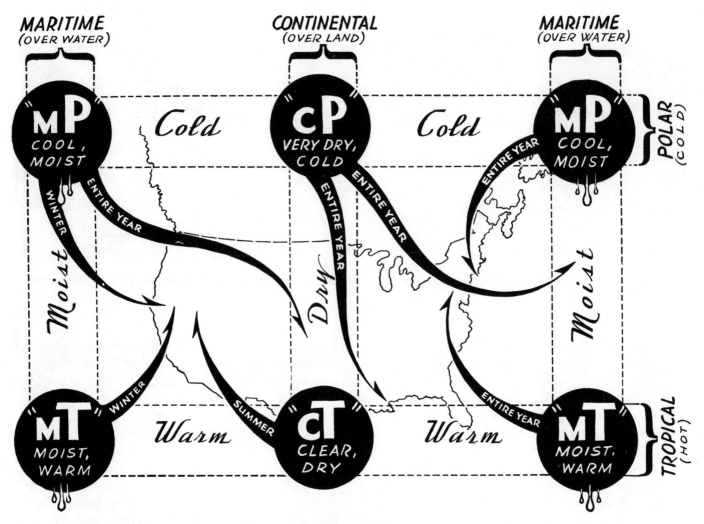

MARITIME (OVER WATER)   CONTINENTAL (OVER LAND)   MARITIME (OVER WATER)

"mP" COOL, MOIST   "cP" VERY DRY, COLD   "mP" COOL, MOIST

POLAR (COLD)

Cold   Cold

WINTER   ENTIRE YEAR   ENTIRE YEAR   ENTIRE YEAR   ENTIRE YEAR

Moist   Dry   Moist

"mT" MOIST, WARM   WINTER   SUMMER   "cT" CLEAR, DRY   ENTIRE YEAR   "mT" MOIST, WARM

Warm   Warm

TROPICAL (HOT)

Drawing 29

maps will feature fronts less as time goes on, and instead will emphasize the masses behind the fronts, naming them, mentioning their characteristics, and giving their predicted weather effects.

Drawing 28 shows a typical cold air mass such as collects in the cold wastes of Canada. Just as the air within your refrigerator is entirely uniform in temperature and wetness and smell and so on, the Canadian air mass grows into a vast bubble of uniform air that periodically bursts. By "bursting," of course, I mean that it loses its mountain confines and overflows into the path of least resistance. By checking with your weather map, you can begin learning to "taste" the bouquet of each new air mass. If you insist that you can "smell the pines or feel the crispness of the northlands" some fresh morning, you will not be talking nonsense. You will be a meteorologist. Check up on your weather map and you will probably find a new flow of cold dry air just down from continental Canada. And you can take the week off to be assured of a few days of clear cool sailing winds and high cumulus cloud puffs. If you can tell what is in your refrigerator by smelling the air inside, you can just as well recognize an air mass by inhaling its atmosphere.

You may learn in time to be an air connoisseur and, like a wine expert who can smell or taste the source of wine, you will be able to sniff air and tell where it came from.

Any material takes upon itself the character-

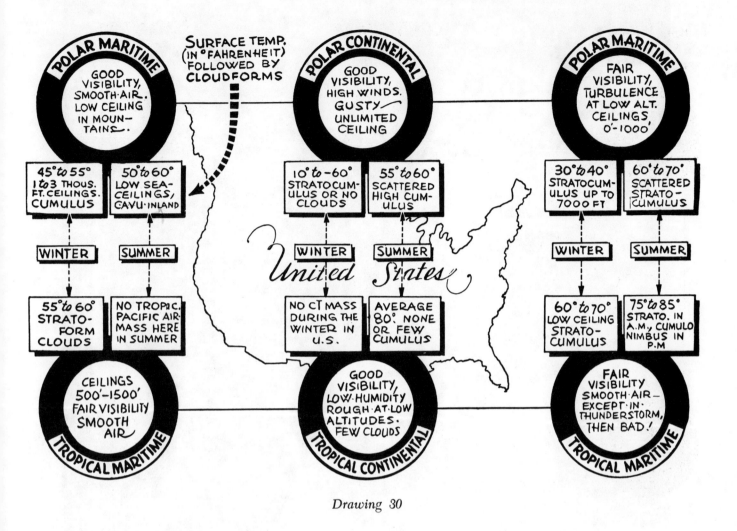

Drawing 30

istics of those things near to it, and this is particularly true of air. Air from cold regions is cold; warm air comes from warm places. Wet air comes from the seas or lakes, while dry air comes from the dry inlands. It's simple, but do remember it.

It wasn't till just a few years ago that we knew about the air masses. Weathermen who were searching for traits in weather found in their records great periodic flows of certain kinds of air. By comparing their qualities with their sources they were found to be cold from the north, warm from the south, wet from the sea, and dry from the inland. And they were tagged *P* for POLAR (cold), *T* for TROPICAL (warm), *M* for MARITIME (wet), and *C* for CONTINENTAL (dry).

Drawing 29 consists of a chart showing the sources and routes of major air masses that affect our weather. The chart, you will observe, is placed over the United States. This arrangement is mathematically simple, for you may see how the wet maritime air (*M*) flows from Atlantic and Pacific sources, while the dry continental (*C*) air comes from the inlands.

Drawing 30 should not be referred to until Drawing 29 has first been thoroughly grasped. It shows the weather effects and visual qualities of each major American air mass. Neither of these charts can be readily memorized, so don't attempt to do so immediately; they will be valuable for reference. By locating strong fronts on your weather map you may check them off from these two charts and decide what temperature and visibility averages to expect for the next day or so.

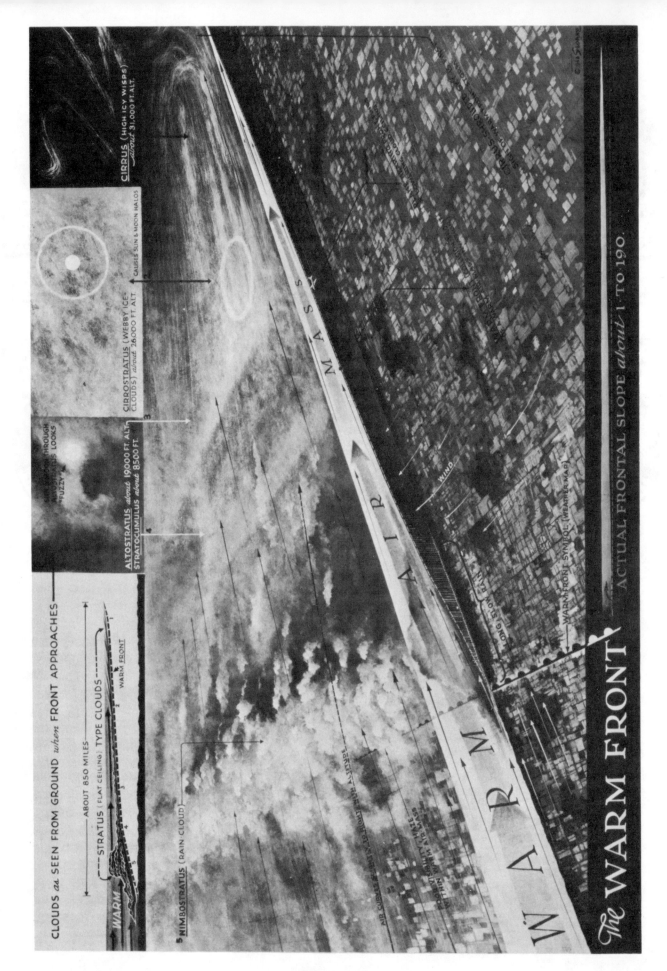

The WARM FRONT   ACTUAL FRONTAL SLOPE *about* 1 TO 190.

Drawing 31

THE WARM FRONT

Like the bright hair uplifted from the head
Of some fierce Maenad, even from the dim verge
Of the horizon to the zenith's height,
The locks of the approaching storm. . . .
— SHELLEY

Drawing 31 shows a cross section through a typical warm front, with the warm air mass moving from left to right. Its frontal surface is marked by a fine white dotted line; notice how delicately slanted is this dotted line. As the front advances, the cloud sequence becomes lower, ending in rain, usually a long but slow sort of precipitation. The black arrows, which show the direction of the air-mass movement, are found veering ever so slightly to the right, in accordance with Coriolis force. The white wind arrows along the ground and just ahead of the front show that the pre-storm wind does not blow from the direction of the oncoming storm at all, but almost at right angles to it. A warm air-mass storm from the south, then, would blow easterly winds in upon New York long before it struck. The final wind shift occurs at the last minute and at the very point where the warm front drags its rainy "tail" along the ground. This drawing may be referred to many times later, but now let us look at a more simplified rendition of the same thing in Drawing 32. Here we have, for variation, shown the warm air mass as seen from the ground and going from the right to the left.

In Drawing 32 we have four sequences of a warm air-mass advance. First, we see a sailor looking upward at the warning sky of CIRRUS. A few scattered mare's-tails overhead are no sign of a storm; in fact, they are a good, healthy fair-weather sign. But when the whole sky becomes clouded with these cirrus webs, that may be regarded as a true warm-front signal. In 2, the sky has lowered a bit and the cirrus has become CIRROSTRATUS, which is heavy, a more solid sky of webs. By 3, the sailor knows that rain is not far off, for the sky has now lowered into ALTOSTRATUS. When the sun or moon shines through altostratus clouds, it becomes shapeless and looks like a ground-glass disk. In 4, the clouds have become low and shaggy NIMBOSTRATUS. Because the warm front leans ahead and flows overhead for a long while before its rainy tail contacts the earth, it is a fine long-range weather forecaster.

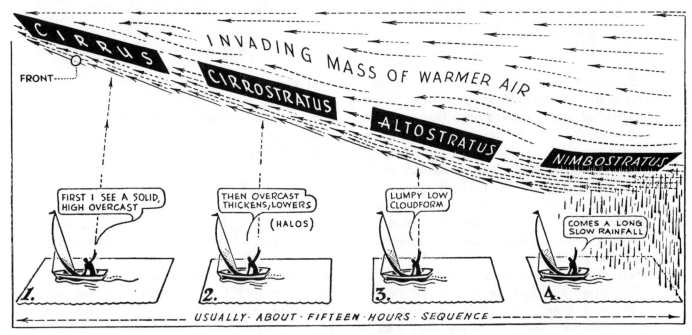

Drawing 32

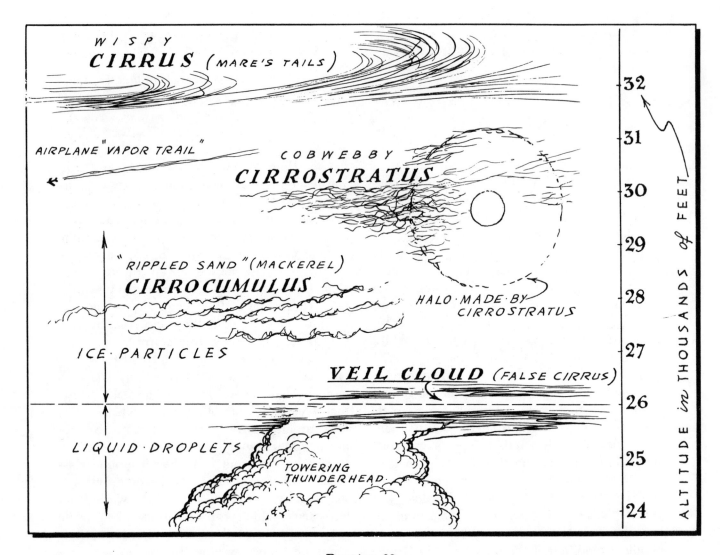

Inside the drawing:

WISPY
CIRRUS (MARE'S TAILS)

AIRPLANE "VAPOR TRAIL"

COBWEBBY
CIRROSTRATUS

"RIPPLED SAND" (MACKEREL)
CIRROCUMULUS

HALO MADE BY
CIRROSTRATUS

ICE PARTICLES

VEIL CLOUD (FALSE CIRRUS)

LIQUID DROPLETS

TOWERING
THUNDERHEAD

ALTITUDE in THOUSANDS of FEET

32
31
30
29
28
27
26
25
24

Drawing 33

Frequently (particularly in summer) the halo around the sun and moon is a good sign of warm air-mass advance. The reason is that when the sun or moon shines through halo-producing cirroform clouds, it is shining through the high nose of a giant warm front. You will notice that the first warm-front cloud warning is cirrus. When the heavens are covered with these icy shreds, you are usually looking at the bow of an invading mass of warmer air. How do you know that such clouds are icy? Their height tells you; over 25,000 feet up all moisture becomes ice because of the intense cold there. All cirroform clouds are composed of ice particles. If you shine a flash-light through a cake of ice or through spun-glass "angel hair" Christmas-tree decorations, you will get a duplicate effect of the warm-front halo.

We shall discuss clouds a little later, but because cirroform or ice clouds are so often connected with the warm front, we might look at Drawing 33 to see the average heights of those webby sky banners which live in a world of constant and intense winter. Because they are ice particles, the question might be raised as to how sheets of ice can hover motionless in mid-air, but the housewife who has seen dust hover in the air can answer that one. Dust is of earth origin, often of heavy meteoric material, yet its smallness in comparison to the slightly ascending fluidness of air keeps it apparently motionless. Incidentally, although cirrus and other high clouds may appear motionless, they exist where the winds average a good seventy-five knots and only their great distance gives the illusion of stillness. Even a jet plane at that height seems motionless.

Like Peter Pan, the ice clouds have no shadow; and the sun and moon shine through them with very little difficulty. However, there will always be a sun or moon halo present, often colored swatches of cloud called "sunbow" and "moonbow." If the sun is shining through two layers of ice cloud, there will be two halos. A halo in winter does not have absolute significance; but during warmer times, usually it is the head of a warm front that pushes cirroform ceilings of warm air overhead; and that, of course, means a lasting rain in about ten hours. Remember the words of the folklore poem, *The moon in halos hid her head?*

Finally you might notice that the clouds associated with a warm air mass are mostly STRATUS or flat in nature. Even lightning, which is unusual with warm fronts, will often assume horizontal tendencies. Cirrocumulus or "mackerel sky" has long been thought a part of warm-front structure and regarded as one of the most reliable signs in folklore predictions. But discard it as a warning. The mackerel sky is liable to appear along *any changing front*. From the first cirrus, to the cirrostratus, the altostratus, and finally the rain clouds, you will usually find that flat dull ceilings and not vertical billow clouds predominate. But the very characteristics of this front make it one of the few recognizable indications that can be depended upon to tell you what tomorrow's weather will be.

ALTITUDE IN THOUSANDS FT.

20

15

10

5

DIRECTION OF STORM

ANVIL TOP FLOWS IN DIRECTION OF STORM

ANVIL TOP

RAIN IS THROWN INTO COLD HEIGHTS FROZEN INTO HAIL, FALLS WHEN HEAVY ENOUGH TO RESIST STORM UPDRAFTS

BUILD-UP OF OPPOSITE POTENTIALS EQUALIZED AS LIGHTNING RELEASE

FRIGORIFIC CLOUDS BECOMING LOWER, DARKER, AND LARGER

"SADDLE BACK" (BLUE SKY) BETWEEN THUNDERHEADS

CUMULO-NIMBUS (THUNDERHEAD)

LINE SQUALL

FRACTO-CUMULUS (SCUD)

GOOD VISIBILITY, HIGH CLOUDS, FAIR WEATHER

COLD AIR MASS

COLD FRONT

TURBULENCE

WARM AIR MASS

AREA INVADED BY COLD AIR MASS

WARM AREA about to be invaded

PRECIPITATION AREA OF COLD FRONT IS NARROW RAIN IS HARD, SOON OVER

COLD FRONT SYMBOL AS SEEN ON A WEATHER MAP

CROSS FRONT at RIGHT ANGLE

The COLD FRONT AS IT APPEARS ALONG THE COLLISION FRONT OF A FAST-MOVING MASS OF UNSTABLE COLD AIR

Drawing 34

8 THE COLD FRONT

His rash fierce blaze of riot cannot last,
For violent fires soon burn out them-selves;
Small showers last long, but sudden storms are short.
— SHAKESPEARE

Drawing 34 shows a mass of colder air moving in from the left and pushing into the warmer, cloud-filled air on the right. As it advances, its snowplow nose of heavy (dense) cold air gets under and pushes up the warm air into violent thunderheads or cumulonimbus forms.

Because of the speed and also the backward slant of a cold front there is not much warning before its entrance, except for its frequent thunder and lightning. Whereas the warm front usually forecasts a lingering rain, the cold front is the broom of the skies, sweeping sultry air away with a quick hard shower and leaving fine crisp air in its wake.

The characteristics of a cold front are its cumulus or lumpy clouds, the cold dry air it brings, its sudden rain, and its speed, which often averages twenty to thirty miles an hour.

The cold front is steeper and faster than the warm front, which it frequently overtakes. When this occurs you will have an OCCLUSION, where the stronger front lifts the weaker one aloft. This overlapping is called an OCCLUDED FRONT, which we shall discuss later in relation to the weather map.

When a warm and cold front collide head-on, the result is a deadlock and a STATIONARY FRONT. Drawing 35 shows the stationary-front mechanics and its map symbols. This front features dull skies and a lingering rain until one air mass or the other becomes strong enough to break a bulge through the frontal line and cause it to decay. An interesting feature to note about the stationary front is that its winds flow parallel but each in an opposite direction to the other.

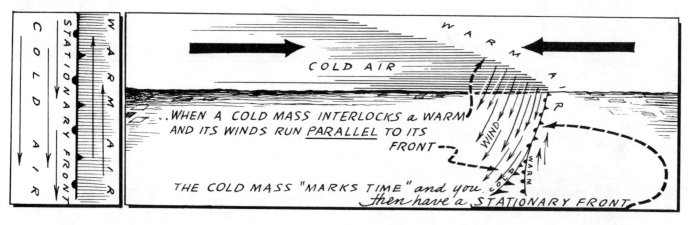

Drawing 35

43

Approach of a Line Squall

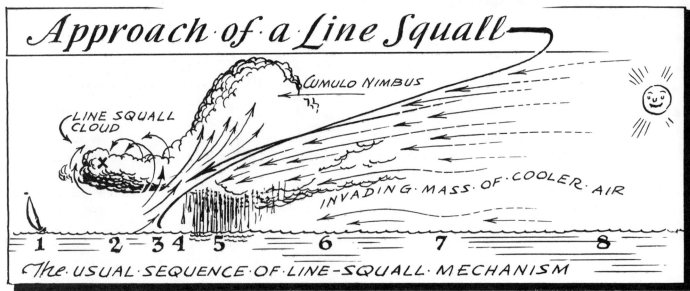

The·USUAL·SEQUENCE·OF·LINE-SQUALL·MECHANISM

I wield the flail of the lashing hail,
And whiten the green plains under;
And then again I dissolve it in rain,
And laugh as I pass in thunder.
— SHELLEY

A line squall is really the front of a front. It is like the fuss kicked up along the front end of a barge, the curling wood shavings that wind up along the front end of a plane's blade, the piling snow in front of a snowplow. When a cold front is fast, its downward snout roots all the warm air in its path, sending it aloft vigorously into a teeming mass of howling black-cloud fury. The winds are seldom less than fifty knots, sometimes approaching eighty.

As shown in Drawing 36, the squall cloud is also the sign of a direct wind shift. The fact that winds in advance of a cold air mass usually flow at right angles to the approaching storm line causes a direct shift when the front passes. With your face to the pre-storm wind (the wind before the front strikes you), you may expect it to shift to your right after the storm has passed. The drawings in 37 show how wind tends to flow along the isobars and in (A) how the wind will shift to your right if you face the wind before a storm.

The speed of the wind depends upon the pressure gradient, and, of course, the closer together the isobars on your map, the greater the wind there. Thus in (B), where the isobars are equally far apart both before and after the storm, the same wind force may be expected in the two air masses. In (C), however, where the isobars are far apart behind the storm and closer together ahead of it, high winds may be expected to change into weaker ones when the storm has subsided. In (D), weak pre-storm winds are shifting into post-storm winds.

The line squall is a cold air-mass machine and,

though it may leave a lot of overturned sailboats and broken sticks in its wake, the weather left behind will be close to perfect. To the lover of sky pageantry, nothing can be more spectacular than a squall cloud. It is the only cloud that boils and tears itself into shreds before the eyes of the beholder without a torrent of rain to spoil the sight. Its blue-black and sulphurous yellow hues are frightening. The turbulence can be actually heard in howls and whines. The rapid change of temperature and electrical potentials will make cloud-to-ground strikes frequent. It's a grand show and one not to be forgotten; the whole program is shown in Drawing 36, and at the top is a sequence that you might care to remember or even to compare when the next squall storm comes your way. At Station 1 the sailorman will either be battening down loose gear or running fast for port. At 2 the black squall clouds will be passing overhead and he will be wondering why it is not raining. At 3 he may even perceive a slight lightening of the sky and wonder if the storm is not going to miss him, after all. But at 4 the wind shift will have struck and, along with the new air mass, the first large drops will begin to fall. At 5 there is a cloudburst type of rain and the thunderhead is directly overhead. At 6 the rain lets up. At 7 the broken scud clouds and fractocumulus pass by, and by 8 the new air mass is well around him and he is in a world of clear, dry, cool air. The show is over and the observer has seen one of the most dramatic productions that Mother Nature puts on.

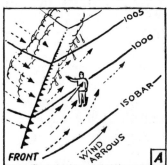 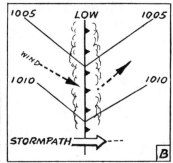 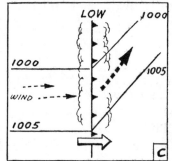 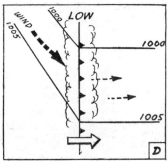

Drawing 37

Men judge by the complexion of the sky
The state and inclination of the day.
— SHAKESPEARE

In Drawing 38 you will behold a complicated mess. Most weather maps are just that, and most people look at them thoughtfully only to look away uninformed. Sometimes you will find it raining right smack in a high-pressure area or the sun shining right in the middle of a low. But the weather map is the basis of all forecasting, and it demands the greatest respect from all weather prophets. It still provides the beginning for any intelligent weather forecast, followed next by the wind direction.

In the middle of the page you will find an average weather-map design. Dotted lines lead from the various features of the map to a thumbnail explanation of each one. This is a page that will take a bit of studying and comparing with your current map, but with some effort the reader will find he can read a weather map from it.

You see a high over the Northwest, and a low toward the middle East Coast. The winds in and around New York are probably high (close isobars) and the rain is fairly heavy (strong low there). But by tomorrow it will all pass out to sea and clear weather will have set in. There is one of each kind of front in this diagram, and you can easily visualize the actions of each. Note, too, how the winds flow clockwise out of the high and counterclockwise into the low. I have used "Indian-type" arrows; the next chapter will explain the wind arrows of Beaufort's scale, which are often used.

The cold front has caught up with the warm front near Cleveland and the whole cyclonic machine at this point will wind itself into a whirlpool-like occluded front of wind and rain within a matter of ten or twenty hours, and wind itself into nothingness within another day or so.

After studying this chart for a while, do look at your daily newspaper map and see what features you can pick out. If you really want to be a weather-map student, snip out a series of maps and chart the course of the weather patterns, for the map, remember, is not a static thing but like a still picture taken from a rather fast-moving set of camera pictures. You need a whole set to conceive the action.

Finally comes a dismaying note. Almost everyone who looks at a weather map forgets that he is looking at a picture of *yesterday's* weather. Or maybe he never even knew it. Frequently he believes that he is looking at tomorrow's weather! If you look at the date on the map you will find that it was compiled some time the day before; the weather picture at the moment will be quite different and the weather tomorrow will be still more different. But as long as you realize that you are looking at yesterday's weather, and if you know the tendencies of weather movements, you can all the better predict what tomorrow's weather (the map of which will be prepared the day after tomorrow) will be like.

It all sounds quite complicated but you can see why the weather map is still the basis for a forecast and also why sometimes the cloud or folklore type of observation (when complemented by your map report) can be very valuable in reaching a decision when the map reading is indefinite.

Let me finish this weather-map story by describing it as a picture of *the trend of the day's atmosphere.* It is like looking at yesterday's stock quotations to determine what will happen today. I think daily weather maps should also include the temperature and conditions that prevailed last year and the year before; possibly they should go back for five or ten years. The figures would be interesting to compare, and would frequently indicate both trends and exceptions.

For two centuries Americans have been convinced that "winters aren't what they used to be." This may be true. In 1780 the winter was so cold that horses and sleighs traveled across the ice regularly between Staten Island and the Battery. Such an instance might be phenomenal, though legends of early New Eng-

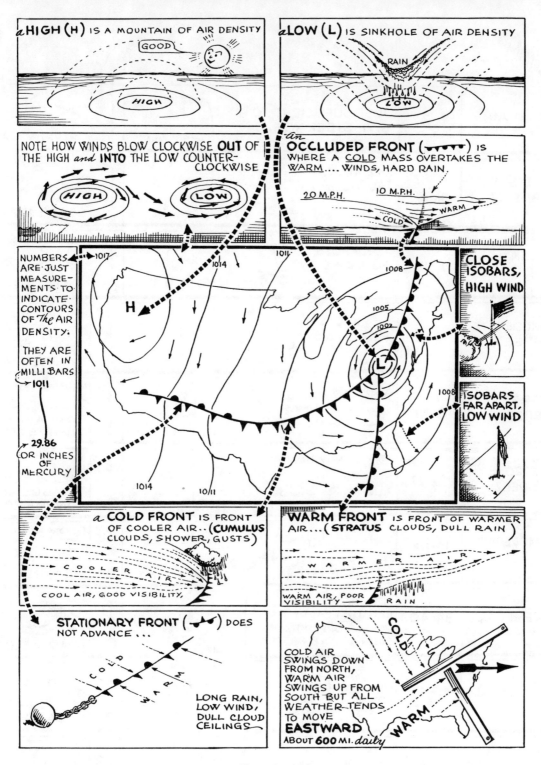

Drawing 38

land describe much colder winters than we have today. Currier and Ives prints show ice-boating clubs on the Hudson River, and one is reminded of the icebreakers that used to clear that river regularly, and the frozen lakes of yesteryear. But the more scientific records show very little difference. As we age we tend to remember the severe winters and to forget the mild ones, because the mind has a distinct tendency to recall the spectacular and to forget the usual. This is one of the reasons why we hear of "old-fashioned winters." One of the pleasures of keeping a diary of weather reports or a scrapbook of daily weather maps lies in making comparisons with today's weather and in noticing trends toward climatic change.

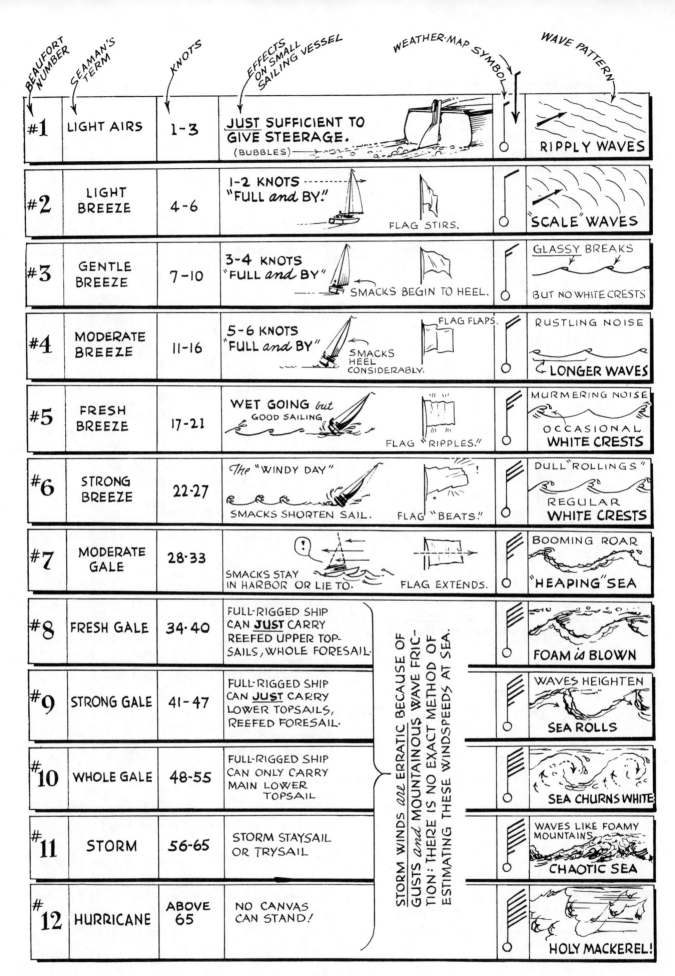

Beaufort Number	Seaman's Term	Knots	Effects on Small Sailing Vessel	Weather-Map Symbol	Wave Pattern
#1	LIGHT AIRS	1-3	JUST SUFFICIENT TO GIVE STEERAGE. (BUBBLES)		RIPPLY WAVES
#2	LIGHT BREEZE	4-6	1-2 KNOTS "FULL and BY." FLAG STIRS.		"SCALE" WAVES
#3	GENTLE BREEZE	7-10	3-4 KNOTS "FULL and BY" SMACKS BEGIN TO HEEL.		GLASSY BREAKS BUT NO WHITE CRESTS
#4	MODERATE BREEZE	11-16	5-6 KNOTS "FULL and BY" SMACKS HEEL CONSIDERABLY. FLAG FLAPS.		RUSTLING NOISE LONGER WAVES
#5	FRESH BREEZE	17-21	WET GOING but GOOD SAILING FLAG "RIPPLES."		MURMERING NOISE OCCASIONAL WHITE CRESTS
#6	STRONG BREEZE	22-27	The "WINDY DAY" SMACKS SHORTEN SAIL. FLAG "BEATS."		DULL "ROLLINGS" REGULAR WHITE CRESTS
#7	MODERATE GALE	28-33	SMACKS STAY IN HARBOR OR LIE TO. FLAG EXTENDS.		BOOMING ROAR "HEAPING" SEA
#8	FRESH GALE	34-40	FULL-RIGGED SHIP CAN JUST CARRY REEFED UPPER TOPSAILS, WHOLE FORESAIL.		FOAM is BLOWN
#9	STRONG GALE	41-47	FULL-RIGGED SHIP CAN JUST CARRY LOWER TOPSAILS, REEFED FORESAIL.		WAVES HEIGHTEN SEA ROLLS
#10	WHOLE GALE	48-55	FULL-RIGGED SHIP CAN ONLY CARRY MAIN LOWER TOPSAIL		SEA CHURNS WHITE
#11	STORM	56-65	STORM STAYSAIL OR TRYSAIL		WAVES LIKE FOAMY MOUNTAINS CHAOTIC SEA
#12	HURRICANE	ABOVE 65	NO CANVAS CAN STAND!		HOLY MACKEREL!

STORM WINDS are ERRATIC BECAUSE OF GUSTS and MOUNTAINOUS WAVE FRICTION: THERE IS NO EXACT METHOD OF ESTIMATING THESE WINDSPEEDS AT SEA.

Drawing 39

11

Every wind has its weather.
— BACON

Once upon a time there was an admiral who invented a fancy scale for indicating velocities of the wind. This happened over one hundred and forty-six years ago and was the sort of thing admirals went around doing in those days. Yet modern weather maps still use the wind scale of Admiral Sir Francis Beaufort, and students repeat the same words set down by his crow quill in 1805. Whether you are jet pilot or sea captain, you will be expected to know your Beaufort's scale, and will be frowned upon by the weather moguls if you refer to wind speeds in miles per hour.

When aviation law required it, I learned the thing by heart to get my flying license; then forgot it immediately with very little effort. It seemed so silly at the time that I began a one-man campaign to install a new system. I started my brave effort by writing to fifty well-known air pilots and weathermen, challenging them to repeat the Beaufort sequence by heart. Believe it or not, none of them knew it!

My own idea of a scale for indicating wind velocity is simple. It uses ten knots per number and five knots per half of a number. Three and a half would thus be thirty-five knots, nine would be ninety knots, and so on. There would be absolutely no memorizing. On weather maps the wind arrow would have two barbs for twenty knots, three and a half barbs for thirty-five knots. A child could read it. Some military maps have adopted this scheme and many airline weathermen use it on their maps.

I contend that no average sailor can tell you the exact speeds of "light," "gentle," "moderate," "fresh," and "strong" winds. Imagine memorizing that Beaufort 9 indicates "chimney pots and slate removed" or that with Beaufort 6 "umbrellas are used with difficulty." I personally do not use an umbrella and I dislike Beaufort's scale.

Drawing 39 shows the new scale with nautical indications which might accompany such wind speeds. Because nothing exactly like it has been done before, there might be some controversy about my interpretation; but at least this presentation is visual and understandable.

Beaufort's scale was designed for use with an anemometer set twenty feet above the surface of the ground, so that estimations of wind speeds at wave heights are liable to be quite inaccurate. Again the movement of a boat itself will distort the estimate. For instance, even the delicate wind-vane at the masthead is not accurate, for the wind direction will be changed by the actual direction and the speed of the vessel.

At sea everything is relative, and the yachtsman's interpretation is liable to be different or at least to be differently worded from the landlubber's. And as time goes on one finds such rich words as "fresh," "rolling," "full and by," to have more defining quality than mere numbers or scientific classification, so one does not take Beaufort too seriously. Tell what sails you used, what sounds you heard, or how your vessel acted, and a sailor will understand far better than by all the wind-speed classifications in the world.

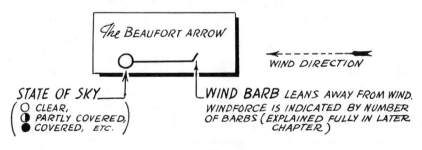

The BEAUFORT ARROW

WIND DIRECTION

STATE OF SKY
(O CLEAR,
  ◐ PARTLY COVERED,
  ● COVERED, ETC.)

WIND BARB LEANS AWAY FROM WIND.
WINDFORCE IS INDICATED BY NUMBER
OF BARBS (EXPLAINED FULLY IN LATER
CHAPTER)

Drawing 40

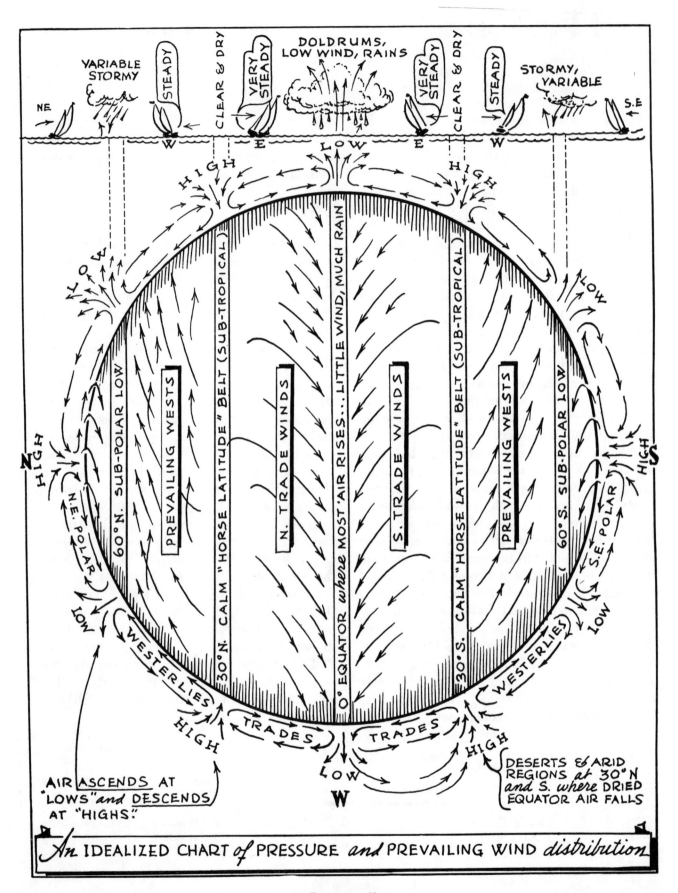

VARIABLE STORMY

STEADY

CLEAR & DRY

VERY STEADY

DOLDRUMS, LOW WIND, RAINS

VERY STEADY

CLEAR & DRY

STEADY

STORMY, VARIABLE

N.E.

W

E

LOW

E

W

S.E

HIGH

HIGH

LOW

LOW

HIGH

HIGH

60° N. SUB-POLAR LOW

PREVAILING WESTS

30° N. CALM "HORSE LATITUDE" BELT (SUB-TROPICAL)

N. TRADE WINDS

0° EQUATOR where most air rises... LITTLE WIND, MUCH RAIN

S. TRADE WINDS

30° S. CALM "HORSE LATITUDE" BELT (SUB-TROPICAL)

PREVAILING WESTS

60° S. SUB-POLAR LOW

N.E. POLAR

S.E. POLAR

N

S

LOW

LOW

WESTERLIES

WESTERLIES

HIGH

HIGH

TRADES

TRADES

LOW

W

AIR ASCENDS AT "LOWS" and DESCENDS AT "HIGHS."

DESERTS & ARID REGIONS at 30° N and S. where DRIED EQUATOR AIR FALLS

An IDEALIZED CHART *of* PRESSURE *and* PREVAILING WIND *distribution*

Drawing 41

It seems that once upon a time a tug operator accepted a delicate towing job entirely upon the predictions of a free-lance weather broadcaster. As things turned out, the weatherman wished he had stuck to the official reports, for the tug and three barges were nicely wrecked. The weatherman was sorry and the broadcasting company was sued. Right or wrong, you cannot sue the United States Weather Bureau, so their report is usually the weatherman's bible.

The tug business seemed a good study for a weather-wise person so I dropped by at the home port of the famous Moran tugboats. What I thought was a business founded on the ability of a fleet of little boats to push things around New York Harbor turned out to be a sort of world-wide navy. Many tugboats are sea-going craft with twelve-foot propellers, towing a two-block long dredge to the Dutch East Indies or pulling an 8500-ton dry dock a thousand miles or more or accomplishing any number of bizarre missions in the far corners of the world.

Winds mean a great deal to such a global business, and I was indeed gratified to see the chart of the old textbook *Winds of the World* (Drawing 41) actually being used. Here are the sea-level winds caused by friction and the movement of the earth. They are not constant but they are so nearly constant that sea routes are mapped by them and, even in this day of engines, the seaman has the greatest respect for the prevailing winds, which feel the best and pile up biggest profits when they are blowing from the stern. The pattern of Drawing 41 holds more true in the Southern Hemisphere, where there is mostly ocean and less land-heat to conflict with the global air design. The belts of calm were as important to avoid in the old sailing days as the prevailing winds were important to follow, and without wind maps like the one we are discussing, the ancient mariners must have had a bad time of it. Notice that the calm belts are calm because all the air there seems to be going upward instead of sideways. It is in these upward winds that you will find lowering clouds and lasting torrents of rain such as seen in the upper cross-section

sketch showing the doldrums.

What a machine is global weather! Squint your eyes and this chart looks not unlike a radial motor; each circulatory cell operates like a separate cylinder, and with mechanical perfection.

It is the movement of air and the resulting weather changes that make life possible.

Drawing 42 shows that the earliest miners were familiar with the air's anatomy and mechanics when they ventilated their mines by heating one end. The rising air created a man-made wind that freshened the air and made living possible down below. The sun's heat and the global winds it creates make up a very similar mechanism.

It is important to note that although the sun heats the air, it does so very indirectly. Atmosphere is like a pane of glass; the sun shines right through it without heating it. For example, the sun will shine through an icy windowpane and make a warm spot inside your room without giving the least bit of heat to the glass. But, in turn, the glass is heated by the warmed room. Just so in nature: it is the sun-warmed earth that heats the air. That is why, by flying just a short way aloft — above thermal circulation — you will find the atmosphere a constant and year-round winter temperature. Funny, isn't it? One would suppose that the nearer he got to the sun the warmer it would be; but no, upper air is frigid. Of course, if there are imperfections in atmosphere, such as dust, the sun will heat the dust particles and, in turn, the air around them will become warm. But for all general purposes of wind and circulation, thermals of rising warm air from the earth are the heat machines.

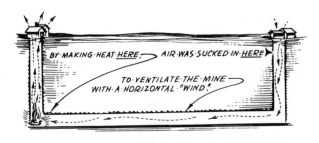

Drawing 42

51

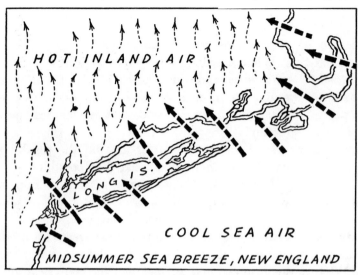

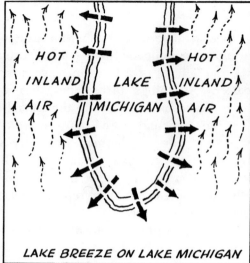

Drawing 43

Most thermals form over land, where the sun's heat saturates the soil and great heat canopies accumulate. For instance, all sailors know how cumulus clouds frequently form continuously over an island, and they are familiar with the old shipwreck rule about rowing toward the part of the horizon where the cumulus clouds are gathered, land usually being there. But thermals do form over open water too, wherever the sea takes on more heat than its surrounding area. As soon as the sun's heat is diminished by a cloud a differential is caused and an immediate thermal circulation occurs. Shallow bodies of water become warm during summer and thermals may be found rising from covered shoals. In calms the racing sailor may find light flows of air moving toward such shoals, to take the place of the rising warm air. Thermals over warm land can suck in so much surrounding air that midsummer breezes become well developed wind systems, such as the summer sea breezes on Lake Michigan and in Long Island (Drawing 43).

The land breeze, of course, is the antithesis of a sea breeze, resulting from after-sunset cooling. Land breezes, however, seldom reach ten miles an hour and are restricted to the immediate coast line. They reach their maximum velocity at about sunrise. In general the land breeze is just an interesting wind, with little practical sailing application because of its weakness and its propensity to be overcome by coast-line wind systems. The only exceptions seem to be such as are found on the shores of Lake Erie between Buffalo and Cleveland where land breezes occur almost regularly each night and early morning.

The sea breeze can be seen to depend upon the sun's heat upon the land. If the sun is partially or totally obscured for a few hours, the breeze to shore will often give way to a calm or to a weak gradient wind. A cloudy day,

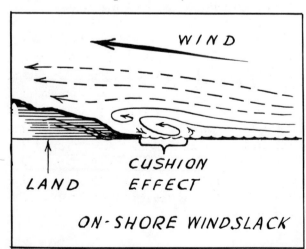

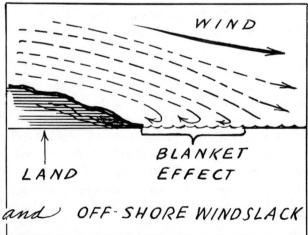

Drawing 44

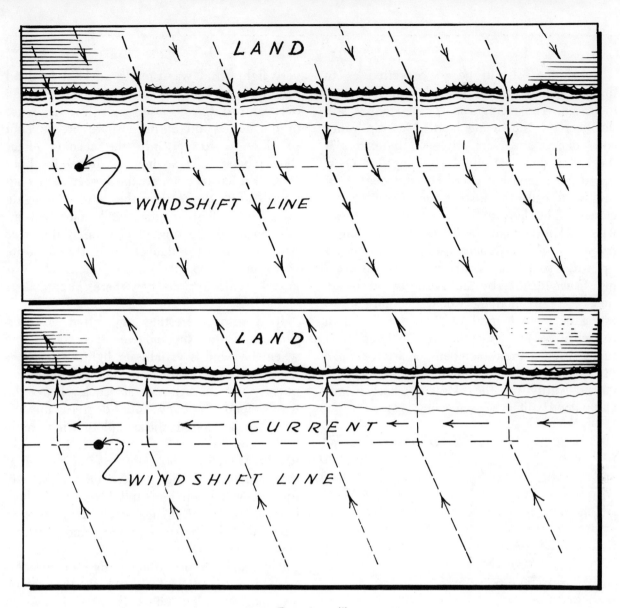

Drawing 45

therefore, will not produce a steady sea breeze. A sailing man can anticipate a diminishing sea breeze when the sky becomes threatened with clouds.

Drawing 44 shows the shoreline anatomy of shore winds, particularly the cushion and blanket effect that sailors avoid along the immediate shore line. In both cases pictured the wind there becomes slack, gusty, and unreliable.

This effect may extend five or six hundred feet outward when the breeze is blowing onshore and about one or two thousand feet outward when the breeze is blowing offshore. In both cases the extent of the cushion and blanket effect can be evidenced by a change in wave structure, and tendency toward calmness or choppiness.

Drawing 45 shows an effect of land and sea breeze that not all sailors know about. When the general wind is not directly onshore or offshore but at an angle, you will find a wind-shift line as you approach the shore, where the wind will change and become more direct, or at right angles to the land. The position of this wind-shift line will depend upon the strength of the wind, but I have often found it to vary between two and three thousand feet from Long Island shores where the sea or land breeze is moderate. Where the shore line varies, look for the sea breeze or land breeze to vary also.

53

No skipper should be so conceited as to think his judgment is better than his wind indicator. The racing vane or pennant is still the heart of the racing boat. Mast-tip vanes and colored streamers are good indicators if the sailor does not mind straining his neck, but the art of using every bit and change of the wind calls for instant and scientific accuracy. The lighter the wind, the more we want to know about it. A yachting cartoonist, trying to be funny, once drew a hollow mast tip with, somehow, a stream of smoke coming from it, thereby indicating wind direction. Actually nothing would be more interesting or more helpful to a good sailor than so sensitive an indicator, for I have seen times when a crew member's cigarette smoke (if not from directly under the boom) has gained yards for the skipper whose wind-vane stood still in a near calm.

We seem to have become quite nautical here, but we are dealing with light and variable surface winds, the sort of thing that mainly interests sailing men. So if you are a landlubber, bear with me; perhaps you'll get around to sailing someday, anyway.

Drawing 46 shows that in spite of a longer course, one air-minded skipper adds speed by utilizing the aiding effect of suction wind as long as he can, and then at a point almost opposite the mark holds straight across the stretch, getting there ahead of the boat that made a crow-flight course through slower-moving air. This is the sort of tactic that makes racing the pleasure that it is. The man on the dotted line has aimed straight to the mark (x), thinking he had the right wind to get him there first. The man on the solid line knew in both cases that the

very light wind was greatly affected by land contours. In the first instance (A) he sped over toward the opposite shore to make use of the added aid of its onshore breeze (not so close as to get into the cushion effect shown back in Drawing 44, but out about 1000 or 1500 feet where the breeze is strongest). In (B) the man on the dotted line again used a crow-flight course, while the weatherwise man on the solid line avoided the wide band of offshore blanket from the opposite shore and utilized the onshore suction he was already enjoying, to get there just a little earlier.

It is also interesting and often advantageous to watch the movements of cloudform when the wind is variable or light. Sometimes there are several directions of wind aloft, frequently not the same as at sea level. As the winds tend to blow four degrees upward from the horizontal, the complete atmospheric body movement will also tend to fall earthward. Therefore the sailor may expect that the direction of the nearest cloudform will soon prevail upon him and his boat if there is to be any wind change at all. He may also, when the sky becomes cloudy and covered, expect any offshore or onshore breeze to slacken and the prevailing puffs soon to come from the direction from which the clouds are moving. This effect is often known as "the lull before the storm." Actually the lull has nothing to do with the storm itself, except for the fact that an onrushing cloud cover has stopped the sun's machinery for making local wind. The new wind direction will be the storm wind shift.

A cloudy day will not operate a strong land and sea wind machine, but when the sun is strong and the general or geostrophic wind is weak, the land breeze and sea breeze come into their own; then the sailor cannot know too much about them. There is very little written about such localized meteorological effects, so the sailor has to depend greatly upon his own observations. The drawings upon these pages, however, are the sort that will be of help, for they explain the little things about aerodynamics that all sailing men most need to know.

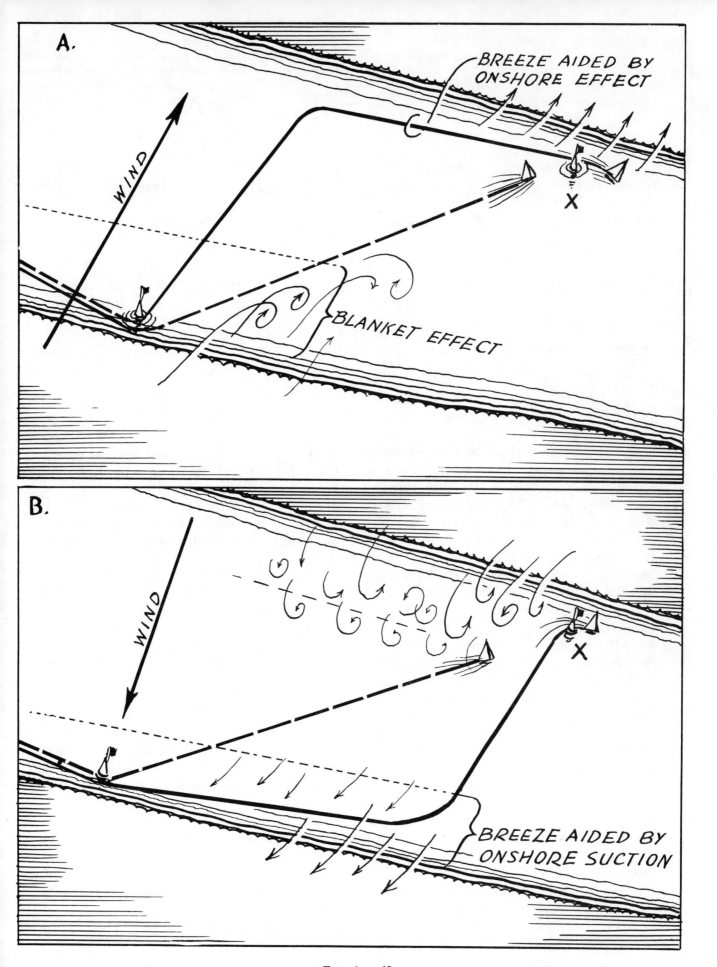

A.

WIND

BREEZE AIDED BY
ONSHORE EFFECT

X

BLANKET EFFECT

B.

WIND

X

BREEZE AIDED BY
ONSHORE SUCTION

Drawing 46

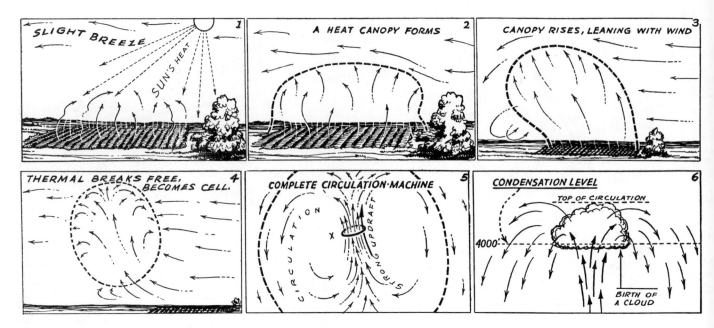

Drawing 47

And now a word about thermal winds, or winds that are actuated by rising warm currents. My *Webster's Dictionary* says that THERMAL means "pertaining to heat" and my meteorology textbook calls it "a cell of rising warm air." The flier knows the thermal as the bump of rising air that pushes him down into his seat. But I like to think of it as a circulatory aerial machine in which as much comes down as goes up: a big doughnutlike arrangement, as shown in Figure 5 of Drawing 47, where the updraft is forced through a small center chimney while the same amount of air falls slowly all around.

Drawing 47 is a set of sketches which depicts the general machinery of a common thermal, from heat canopy to free cell and then to its final dissipation, or if the air is that moist, to the birth of a cumulus cloud. The cumulus cloud, by the way, would be better named the THERMAL CLOUD, for it is really the visible head of a thermal machine, as shown in Figure 6. As you sail beneath these fair-weather cauliflower puffs, do realize that beneath each is the doughnutlike machinery shown, and that the flat bottom shows the level where the air became cold enough to condense into cloudform.

When you think of a thermal you usually think only of rising air. But the old saying that whatever goes up must come down still holds true. With a thermal cell, the same amount of air goes up as comes down but, because of the doughnut shape, the ascending air squeezes necessarily very rapidly through the doughnut hole and dissipates slowly and downward all around it. Therefore an airplane hardly notices the thermal's downdrafts but is jarred uncomfortably by the fast updrafts.

All over the landscape, and the seascape too on a hot day, there are earth-hugging masses of warmed air like the canopy shown in Figures 2 and 3 of Drawing 47; they later balloon up into thermal cells, as shown in Figure 4 of the same set of drawings.

Where the sea is dotted with masses of warm air, if the warm air were colored red the effect would be like an expanse of red barrage balloons moored close to the surface. The true wind would be squeezing between these "obstructions" as gusts. Remember this fantastic but enlightening picture when you fly over open water, for you will see long ruffled streaks moving irregularly but with the wind, making a regular pattern of CAT'S-PAWS over the sea's surface.

Although every sailing man or child knows

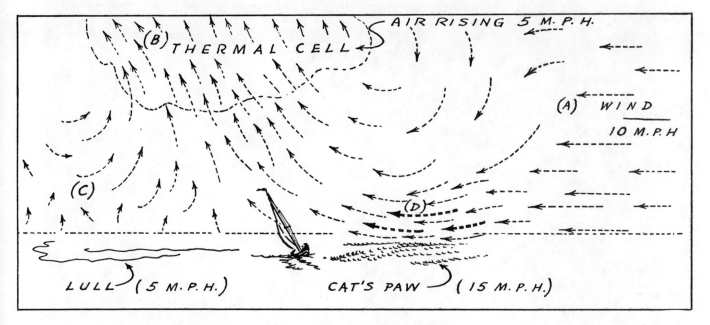

Drawing 48

these cat's-paws that ruffle the surface of calm water, I have never seen a satisfactory explanation of them. So, because I can always go back to painting if the slide-rule meteorologists frown too severely at me, I have devised my own explanation — shown in Drawing 48.

Any small variation in a light wind, or a light wind that breaks a calm, is known as cat's-paw. Sailors have learned to call the resulting flurry on the water's surface a cat's-paw, watching eagerly for them in order to detect an occasional gust. Gusts are the characteristic of all winds, from the sea and land breezes to the hurricane. But because we are discussing sea-level thermals, we will consider the relationship between gusts and thermals.

Ordinary winds have a velocity variation of about 50 per cent and a direction variation of about 25 per cent. Of course, such variations are of extreme interest to operators of sail-driven vessels. Even a cat's-paw can win a trophy. Gustiness is more prevalent when a strong horizontal wind is penetrated by many thermal cells, such as the one shown in Drawing 48. Here we see a light wind (A) and a drifting thermal (B) which contains air rising at about five miles an hour. Ahead of and below the cell you will experience a slight lull (C) such as you get before the cat's-paw (D), which consists of the true wind plus a five-mile-an-hour movement to replace the rising cell's volume. There is no way to anticipate such gusts, for thermal cells are, of course, quite invisible. When the wind is blowing off warmed land, however, you may expect to sail by gusts or you may move to sea where the thermals are higher or more dissipated. By looking at the drawing you may see why the top of a high sail will often be touched by the gust before you feel its brush down near the water's surface.

Yes, there are as many vertical winds as there are horizontal ones. We do not feel them at sea level, but we get their effects, either in cloudform or in gusts. I like to call them "the winds that go up and down."

Drawing 49

12   THE WORLD OF CLOUDS

I am the daughter of Earth and Water,
And the nursling of the sky;
I pass through the pores of the oceans and shores;
I change, but I cannot die.

                           — SHELLEY

If an occasional rain were sent across the sky to water the ground below, the purely utilitarian purpose of clouds would be fulfilled. But when we behold the unending panorama of cloud beauty which seems to form for no reason but to be the countenance of Nature and the backdrop for our daily life, we are apt to assume that fair-weather clouds exist merely for our pleasure to behold. Actually there are many other reasons besides rain for clouds, even though clouds seem to come from the air and go back again without having accomplished a purpose. We have discussed how weather is the result of an uneven heating of the earth. Well, as shown in Drawing 50, clouds reflect back much of the sun's rays and thereby set up a machinery of weather that keeps small areas circulated horizontally.

Clouds may not seem to be much of a parasol from the sun on a fine day because daylight can be so indirect that we don't notice their shade, but when next you go up in an airplane, look

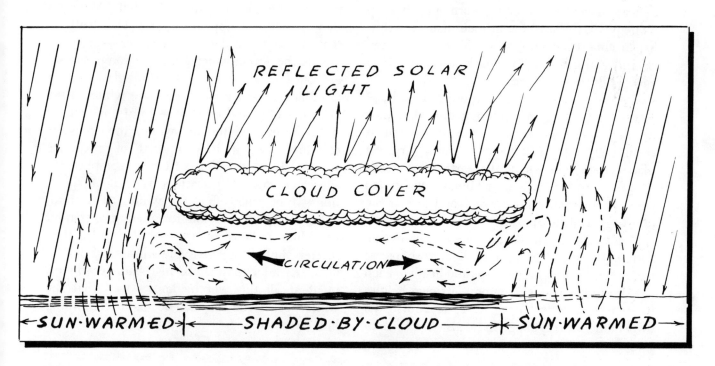

Drawing 50

down and you will see the landscape mottled with big splashes of shade from more clouds than you thought were up there with you. When you realize that each area of shade is a circulation machine moving over the earth even faster than low-level winds, you can see what a maze of circulatory machines combs the earth. Each circulatory cell becomes a potential machine for making another cloud, so we have the picture of one cloud dropping eggs of shade to give birth to other clouds in its wake. There is something beautifully alive in these heavenly shapes that are born from the atmosphere and disappear noiselessly back again with the grace of ballet dancers. Shelley caught the cycle of cloud life when he made his cloud speak, saying, "I change, but I cannot die"; then, later, "And out of the caverns of rain, Like a child from the womb, like a ghost from the tomb, I arise, and unbuild it again."

You have probably never thought of clouds moving gracefully because they gyrate more slowly than our senses can perceive. Their only noticeable movement seems to be their horizontal speed as they move with the wind. But if you wish to be fascinated — almost hypnotized — by movement, watch a speeded-up motion picture of a cloud forming and dying. It is like a magnificent flower being born, pushing up white petals the size of apartment houses, writhing in almost animal ecstasy till it has reached its full stature. Its flow back into the air is an equally fine spectacle.

The obvious utilitarian purpose of clouds, of course, is to be giant watering pots that pick up moisture from one place and deposit it at another. They take water up from very wet places, then rain where the earth most needs it. Dry land has an almost human capacity to reach its thermal arms upward and loosen the rain trigger of low passing clouds.

The world of clouds is a very precise one. Although many of us think of them as shapeless white puffs that occur spasmodically, each cloudform has its own anatomy, its own height, its own reason for being, and, of course, its own name. Everything, it seems — even neb-ulous wisps of cloud — has its place in this orderly universe.

Anatomically, there are only three kinds of clouds to remember: lumps (CUMULUS); layers (STRATUS); and icy (CIRRUS). You puff a cigarette cloud of CUMULUS shape; if you smoke enough there will be a STRATUS cloud shape hovering in the room. If you open the Deepfreeze, you will see wisps of CIRRUS curl out. These shapes can be seen in the upper part of Drawing 49, while a composite chart of all the clouds is depicted below. Notice that the names cumulus, stratus, and cirrus are further qualified by Latin words like ALTO for high, NIMBUS, for head, and so on. Their average heights are shown on the left side in thousands of feet, and each cloud name is followed by a two-letter weather-map designation. The heights of clouds depend upon latitude, as we have already mentioned, but also upon the time of year. Summer clouds are higher, because the earth then radiates more heat and the atmospheric circulation rises to greater heights. As an artist, I have often had a weather-wise person catch me in the mistake of painting towering summer clouds above a winter snow scene.

Clouds are presumed to be white. At least they certainly look white. A frequent question is not why clouds are white but "Why do they sometimes appear dark?" The truth is that clouds are as colorless as water — as colorless as the water which they are composed of, as colorless as glass. Yet grind glass up, or sandblast it, and it becomes pure white. Take clear ice, also, and crush it — presto, it's white! Actually our whitest of white, the snow, is colorless, too; it is composed of clear ice shapes. It is just the matter of complicating a surface so that it scatters light in all directions; then the effect is white. The individual droplets of cloudform are transparent but, like billions of tiny glass beads, they scatter sunlight to give the illusion of whiteness. A sailor may shake his head in wonderment at all this, yet he knows well that the whitecaps of the sea can be made of nothing but clear water.

60

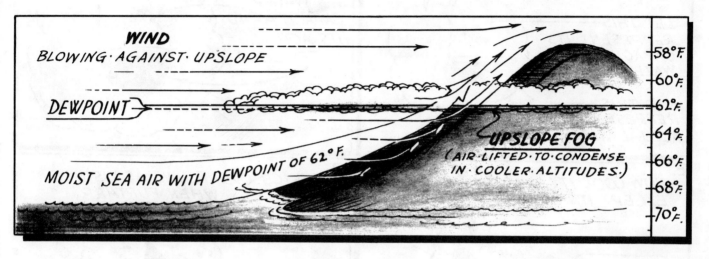

Drawing 51

Clouds become dark when the sunshine is blotted out from their vicinity, but frequently they reflect back the darker colors of earth. I have often seen green-blue clouds reflecting the brilliance of southern seas. Most interesting to the artist or photographer is the reversal of earth color-theory as it exists in the sky. On earth, as with mountains, nearby things have red hues while distant objects become bluer. Faraway mountains, for instance, are almost lost in their blue haze. But in the sky it is different: nearby clouds are bluest, distant clouds are reddest. You will often see thunderous cloud mountains looming sullenly over the horizon like sultans with large red turbans. In fact, the whole horizon is marked by a tinge of distant reddish hues.

Drawing 51 brings us to the elementals of cloudbirth and it deals with something called DEWPOINT. You might think that, because a cloud is wet and white, the air around it is dry. The secret is that moisture can be visible or invisible; when it is gas you *can't* see it; when it is liquid you *can* see it. And cloudbirth is the process of changing moisture from gas to liquid. Evaporation changes moisture back from liquid into gas.

Please let me state that again:

A cloud is the air's moisture gone from invisible gas to visible water droplets.

As you cannot see the water that is hidden in a wet towel, you cannot see the atmospheric water that is in your room; but if you squeeze the towel (shrink it or condense it into a smaller size) the water will then become visible. Likewise, if you can shrink the air in your room (condense it), water droplets will appear, first on your walls and windowpanes and on other cool objects. By shrinking air, you sort of wring the vapor out of it into visible form. That is an unscientific and possibly inaccurate simile, I know, but I hope it puts over an otherwise difficult-to-explain process.

61

Drawing 52A

Look at Drawing 52A and notice how warm air (A) expands in proportion to its capacity for carrying moisture (B). Notice then that, when the capacity or container shrinks (C), the moisture overflows into fog or steam or the water droplets on your cold drink or any of the other forms of visible condensation. When you exhale your warm breath, wet from the inside of your body, and it strikes the cold outside world, your very breath becomes visible. At least the moisture in it does. When the hot damp air of a teapot flows out into the cooler kitchen, its moisture too is cooled and squeezed into visible steam.

So when warm, wet air arises away from the heat of earth to become cooled in the cold heights, it becomes chilled and condenses into visible cloud droplets. All clouds are the result of some sort of cooling. The wetter the

air, the less cooling is needed. Dry air produces no clouds, or else very high ones.

The lowest form of cloud is ground surface air cooled into aerial pools of water known as "fog." There are three ways that fog can form, or three ways that ground surface air can be cooled, as shown in Drawing 52B. First you see ADVECTION FOG, which is caused by warm air flowing over and being cooled by cold ground (1). RADIATION FOG (2) is usually caused by the earth losing heat into the night air, thereby cooling the air directly above it. Cooled air becomes heavier and flows downhill like water, to settle into valleys as fog. When you fly over a countryside of warm wet atmosphere at sundown you will see white patches of radiation fog that look like hundreds of little ponds; these are the cool valleys.

Advection fogs have two variations, the

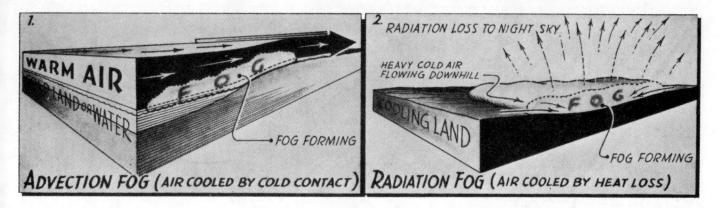

Drawing 52B

STEAM FOG and the UPSLOPE FOG. The steam fog occurs when the opposite action to that shown in Figure 1 happens —cold air flowing over warm surface. This is also known as "frost smoke" or "arctic sea smoke." Because the water is much warmer than the air the evaporation is so intense that steam pours forth from the water and fills the air with fog. This fog is shallow and rare. It is simulated when a hot pavement is hosed during the summer. You have probably seen the steam rise from such a wet sidewalk.

Upslope fog is caused when moist sea air is blown against hills and cooled by being lifted into colder heights. You find upslope fogs in Pennsylvania and along any coastal hill area. The process is shown in Drawing 51 where you see wet ocean air cooled until it reaches its dewpoint by lifting it to colder heights. A heavy wind would dissipate such a fog but a very slow and steady wind will feed fog until it is thick and persistent.

Fogs are more frequent on the Pacific Coast than on the Atlantic, due to the prevailing west-to-east wind. On the East Coast the prevailing wind sweeps off the land and is therefore less humid. However, the moist winds from the Gulf Stream areas do frequently blow upward to the Labrador current in the vicinity of Newfoundland to create a great fog-breeding place. Again, prevailing eastward winds over England carry moisture to soot-laden air to make the thick London fogs. Each soot particle

is a center of condensation, a nucleus for one drop of moisture. The fogs of large manufacturing cities are greatly increased by particles of soot issuing from the chimneys. When smoke and fog mix you get what is known as "smog."

We have discussed fogs as air-cooled by advection and radiation, almost neglecting PRECIPITATION FOG. This is caused by relatively warm rain or snow falling through cold air. When a storm moves in on very cold and wet air the precipitation falls into chilling air, raising the dewpoint and causing fog.

Sailors have little comment about fog but landsmen have some:

> *A summer fog for fair,*
> *A winter fog for rain,*
> *A fact most everywhere,*
> *In valley and on plain.*

and:

> *When fog goes up the rain is o'er,*
> *When fog comes down 'twill rain some more.*

A New England saying goes:

> *Evening fogs will not burn soon,*
> *Morning fog will burn 'fore noon.*

and:

> *Fog that starts before the night*
> *Will last beyond the morning light.*

When fog begins to break up by wind shift, or to burn away from a rising sun, the effect is often strange. I recall paddling out to a duck blind in the early hours while the new day's wind wrapped the fog into columns about six feet high. Thousands of these ghost-

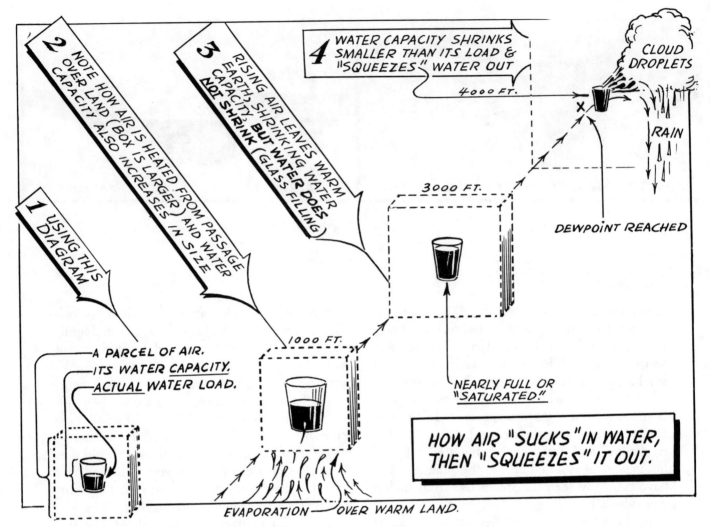

2 NOTE HOW AIR IS HEATED FROM PASSAGE OVER LAND (BOX IS LARGER) AND WATER CAPACITY ALSO INCREASES IN SIZE

3 RISING AIR LEAVES WARM EARTH, SHRINKING WATER CAPACITY, **BUT WATER DOES NOT SHRINK** (GLASS FILLING)

4 WATER CAPACITY SHRINKS SMALLER THAN ITS LOAD & "SQUEEZES" WATER OUT

CLOUD DROPLETS

4000 FT.

X

DEWPOINT REACHED

RAIN

3000 FT.

1 USING THIS DIAGRAM

1000 FT.

A PARCEL OF AIR.
ITS WATER <u>CAPACITY</u>.
<u>ACTUAL</u> WATER LOAD.

NEARLY FULL OR "SATURATED."

HOW AIR "SUCKS" IN WATER, THEN "SQUEEZES" IT OUT.

EVAPORATION — OVER WARM LAND.

Drawing 53

like figures, leaning in the direction of their march, moved silently over the water.

Drawing 52A shows graphically how the air shrinks and overflows into fog. The process of clouds forming aloft is quite the same, except that rising warm air sucks in moisture and thereby becomes lighter and rises faster. So, repetitious, may I call attention to another condensation diagram, this time using a glass to represent the air's water-capacity (Drawing 53). Notice that the air (dotted lines) expands with the lower pressure of altitude while the glass shrinks with the cold. At four thousand feet the glass overflows — and you see the birth of a cumulus cloud. With this action you have a full cycle of Nature: evaporation from the land, which is carried aloft by its own lightness (moist air is lighter than dry); the formation of clouds; and then the dropping of water back again to earth, as rain. Each second, more than sixteen million tons of water pass into the atmosphere through evaporation; and even the smallest summer shower involves hundreds of thousands of tons of water. So the process is a gigantic one, although it operates quietly and invisibly.

Aircraft weather maps indicate the present temperature along with the dewpoint of the present air, such as "Temp. 80°, dewpoint 70°." This would indicate that the present air contains that much moisture so that it needs exactly ten degrees cooling before it will become saturated and close to precipitation. Of course, the greater the spread between temperature and dewpoint, the farther away is rain.

Many people think that "dewpoint" is a term referring to the dew instead of being a humidity and forecasting measurement, so they need to get clear in their minds what dew is. Dew does not fall. It collects on objects colder than the air itself. The moisture that runs down the side of an iced drink is a perfect example of dew. The cold glass has collected water directly from the air in the room.

Because warm air can hold in suspension a larger quantity of moisture than cold air, the cooling of air with the fall of night makes some of its moisture condense in the form of dew. If the temperature is below freezing, however, this collection will be frost rather than dew.

Dew forms more rapidly when the air is calm than when it is in motion. It forms on cloudless nights because there are no clouds to hinder heat radiation. Hence when dew collects there is a clear sky and the morrow will be without rain. A dewless night or early morning is a forerunner of rain.

Another rain forecaster is the well-known castle-with-the-door from which appears either two children or an old witch. The witch means bad weather. There are many variations of this contraption but the first and reliable ones worked upon the same principle as the modern hygrometer, using strands of human hair. Human hair (blond is best) seems to react consistently and accurately to humidity.

Drawing 54(B) shows the dry-and-wet-bulb theory. One thermometer measures the air's temperature. The other is kept wet and measures through the coolness of evaporation the dewpoint or temperature of the same air when saturated. Here again the greater the spread or difference between the two temperatures the farther off is probable precipitation. Sometimes the dry-and-wet-bulb arrangement is mounted on a base with a handle that enables it to be swung around the head, which is called a sling-psychrometer. Each dry-and-wet-bulb thermometer is sold with a chart that enables one to determine by the spread the exact relative humidity.

The hair hygrometer as shown in Drawing 54 (A) measures the degree of saturation of the air, but at low temperatures its lag and inaccuracies recommend that a dry-and-wet-bulb hygrometer be used instead (B). This instrument depends upon the cooling effect of evaporation on a mercurial-type thermometer. By comparing this thermometer with a standard dry one, the spread between dewpoint and actual temperature is established, also how near the air is to the saturation point. The principle is like wetting one of two fingers and holding them aloft to compare the temperatures. The moistened finger will feel coldest. The clearer the day, the greater will be the difference in temperatures between the two fingers, or the great humidity-temperature spread.

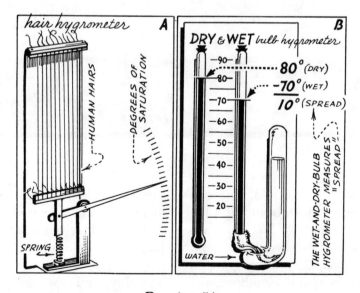

Drawing 54

BIRTH·OF·A·CLOUD (CUMULUS)

WHICH·IS·THE·VISIBLE·HEAD·OF·A·THERMAL

CONDENSATION·LEVEL

THE COOLED AIR, OF SHADED AREAS [A]
AND THE SHOAL-WARMED PLACES [B]
SET UP A CIRCULATORY CELL [C]

WARM AIR CONDENSING

4000 FEET

3000 FEET

2000 FEET

1000 FEET

SEA·LEVEL

(A)
COOLED AIR (SHADE)

(B)

(C)

SHOAL

Drawing 55A

As with all meteorological books, this one has a chapter starting with a beautiful title, "The World of Clouds," but we find ourselves discussing condensation, psychrometers, and hygrometers. For a change I have grouped our cloud knowledge in visible cloudform design in the two-page Drawing 55 A and B,

Birth of a Cloud. Admittedly, this is a pleasant picture that has been cluttered up with arithmetic; but it is quite informative. On the left (A) you see altitudes in thousands of feet; this particular day seems to have an average humidity and the dewpoint occurs at four thousand feet. That line, as you see, marks

66

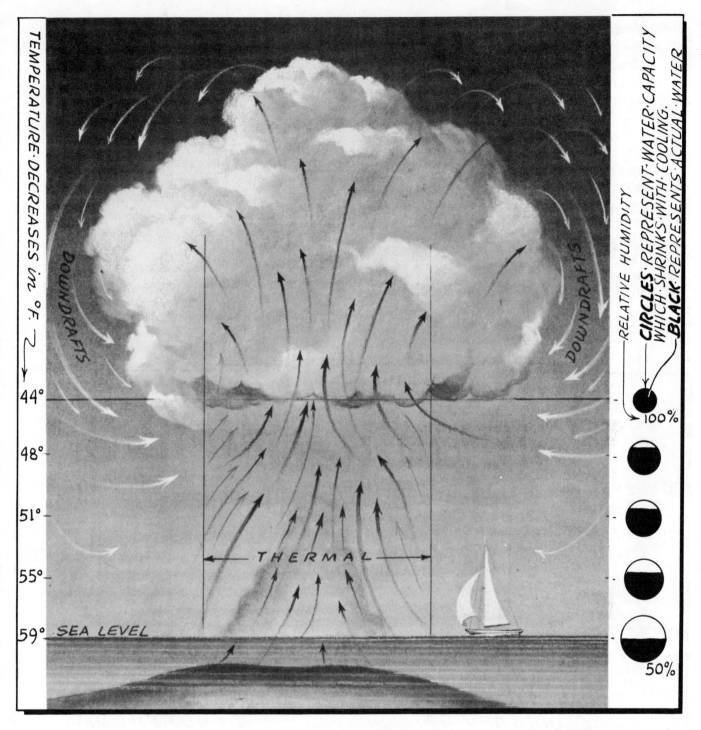

Drawing 55B

the bottoms of all the cumulus clouds "today."

The white arrows indicate the cool air and the dark arrows show the warm air. You see circulatory atmospheric cells beginning over shaded cool areas and over warm shoals. The second drawing (B) shows the full-grown cumulus, with downdrafts spilling over the top and feeding the cloud again from the bottom. Notice that the relative humidity at sea level this day is 50 per cent and naturally the relative humidity at dewpoint height (4000 ft.) will be 100 per cent. It's a good drawing to take along with you when you are lolling on the deck, cloud

67

observing; perhaps it will help you to get the action of clouds and feel their gyrations.

Clouds are always doing something, are always in the process of construction or disintegration. Their appearance of quietness and serenity — actually the effects of slow motion and great height — is misleading. I have flown beside thunderheads that appear solid and motionless from the ground but close at hand look like a boiling caldron with a thousand unseen demons shoveling snow out into the surrounding atmosphere.

The LENTICULAR CLOUD, so called because it usually is in the shape of a lens, seems particularly quiet, because it refuses even to sail with the wind. Perhaps everyone has seen such a fine white cloud hovering high in one spot for the whole day and has presumed that up there the wind must have died down to a calm. Of course the higher you go the less earth friction there is and the more knots there are to wind speed, so you can be assured that the cloud is doing something to maintain its position. Its secret — as shown in Drawing 56 — is that it is continually growing at the windward edge and melting away at the leeward. It may be compared to a waterfall which always stays put, although the water of which it is a part is continually entering at one end and leaving at the other.

This explains why islands over the horizon are marked by a telltale crown of apparently

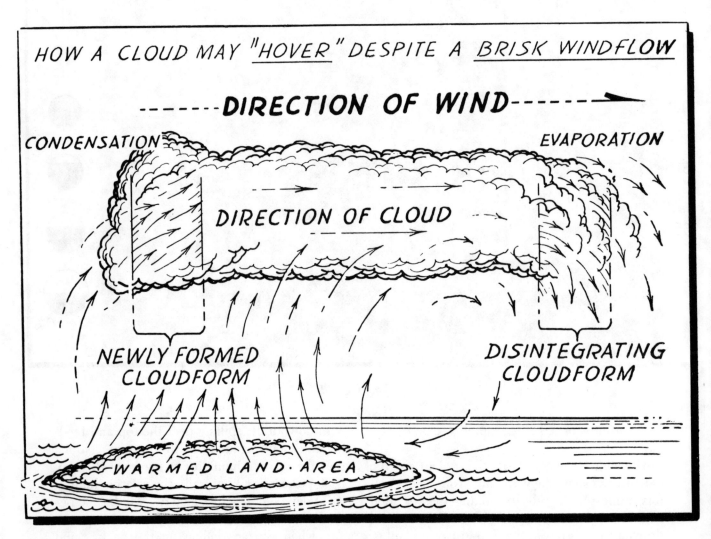

HOW A CLOUD MAY "HOVER" DESPITE A BRISK WINDFLOW

--------- DIRECTION OF WIND -------→

CONDENSATION

EVAPORATION

DIRECTION OF CLOUD - - -→

NEWLY FORMED CLOUDFORM

DISINTEGRATING CLOUDFORM

WARMED LAND AREA

Drawing 56

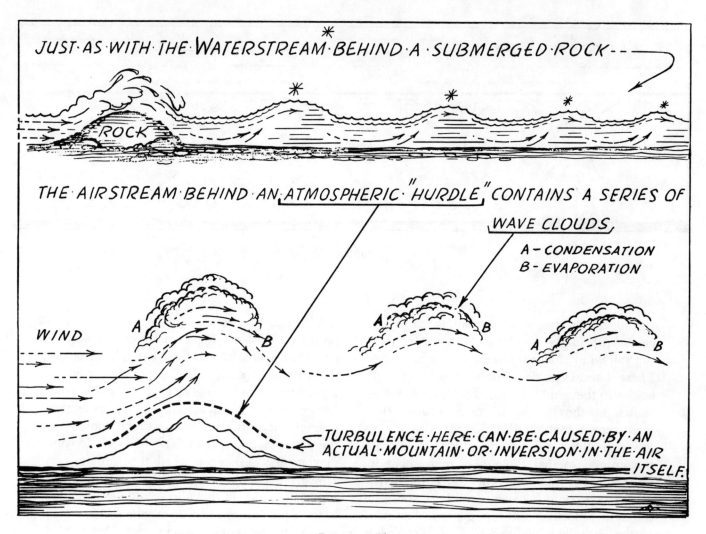

Drawing 57

stationary clouds. Actually they are being condensed by the updraft of warmed air on the windward side of the land and evaporating on the leeward side where the air descends to flow onshore and replace the rising thermals. The same effect may be observed when there is a scarf-cloud standing "still" atop some high mountain peak, or as an abrupt cloud definition following the coast line. When clouds are thick over the land but disappear above the water, look for a strong onshore breeze, for the disappearance of those clouds is caused by a sharp downdraft of replacement air flowing inland to replace the rising currents.

Frequently a series of stationary clouds will be found in a wave formation, trailing in the lee of a warmed city, a mountain, or some other atmosphere-disturbing element. The first part of Drawing 57 compares this phenomenon with a boulder in a swift-moving stream and the presence of leeward waves. There is not only one wave above the boulder but a succession of waves downstream, one after the other. Often there will be a stationary cloud far behind a mountain peak, probably settling high above the leeward valley, yet caused entirely by the long wave behind the mountain. Most famous is the MOAZAGOTL CLOUD which persistently hangs over the center of the valley between the Riesen Gebirge and Hirschberg in the Sudeten Mountains. Glider pilots have reached tremendous heights by soaring on this visible "long wave" just as a surf rider glides with the surf wave.

69

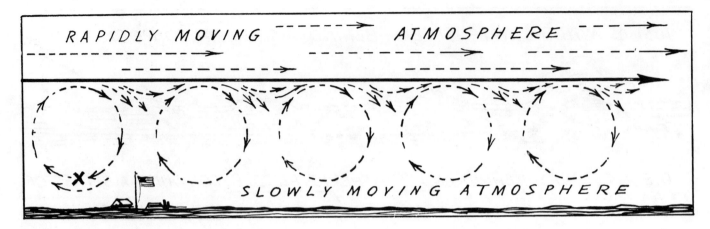

Drawing 58

The clouds described are single, or a succession of single clouds, and do not refer to the roll wind clouds often seen on a brisk day. These banners which extend nearly at right angles to the wind are caused by the mechanics shown at the bottom of these pages. It is well known that, as the air moves along, its lower portions are retarded by friction with the ground so that the rate of movement increases with greater height above the earth. Internal friction between any two strata of different velocities sets up a vertical stirring of the air called "eddy motion" or turbulence, whereby the swifter moving air gets ahead of the retarded parts below, causing rolls and gusts of wind. The bottoms of roll clouds mark the level at which a sharp difference in wind velocity occurs. In Drawing 58, (A) represents fast-moving atmosphere, a sort of jet stream which causes the friction layer nearer the earth to "steamroller" over and over. A logical person will observe in this drawing what seems to be an impossibility. The lower portion of each "wheel" seems to be moving in the direction opposite to that of the whole wind movement. (I have marked this with an x.) However, if a wagon wheel in action is imagined (a diagram of that also would deceive), the bottom portion of the wagon wheel also would appear to be moving backwards. Actually it is only moving slower (in reference to forward action) than the top.

Drawing 59 is really (B) of 58, for it shows the steamroller atmosphere's cloud formation.

Drawing 59

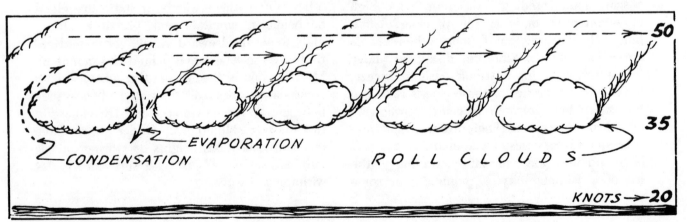

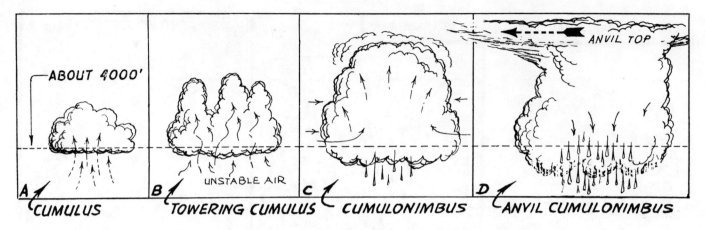

ANVIL TOP

ABOUT 4000'

UNSTABLE AIR

A CUMULUS | B TOWERING CUMULUS | C CUMULONIMBUS | D ANVIL CUMULONIMBUS

Drawing 60

Each roll upward, constantly feeds the condensation machinery while each downward roll feeds that of evaporation. Hence the windy rolls of cloud to be seen are not solitary figures being moved from one place to another. Each roll is being born again and again as it moves with the wind.

Few sights are more ominous than that of a glowing thunderhead over the horizon. Even a hurricane gives a warning, with a cirrus canopy sign a day or so ahead of its whirlpool center, but thunderheads can appear quickly in a clear sky. They move faster than a sailing ship, and the higher they build up the harder will be the rainfall beneath. They are the air pilot's forbidden territory and the yachtsman's invitation back to port. The thunderhead's only blessing is its concentrated area. It is small enough to fly around by air and its path is so narrow that it may miss you by land or sea. I can think of no other cloudform more interesting to behold and study. Information concerning it is sailing or flying insurance, possibly life insurance.

All clouds of the cumulus type are CONVECTIVE, which means they are formed by vertical air currents. Their flat bottoms indicate the altitude at which the air's moisture became cold enough to condense into visible droplets. The higher the cumuli, the drier is the atmosphere and the less possibility there is

of rain. Drawing 60 shows several stages of cumulus forms.

Because "cumulus" suggests "accumulation," it is easy to remember that all lumpy clouds are cumulus types. Fair-weather cumulus clouds as in Diagram 60 (A) are simply the visible heads of thermals which form over heated land or sea to become aerial circulation machines lasting for about a half-hour. But in very unstable air these machines often become a factory of circulation that refuses to dissipate, building up into a towering head known as "cumulonimbus" or "thunderhead." It is possible with practice to forecast summer weather for a few hours ahead by looking at the cumulus clouds and observing their development, particularly the upper parts. If there are no towers on cumulus clouds like those shown in (B) there is less chance of storm. This towering effect is also likened to turrets or castles, hence the name CUMULUS CASTELLATUS.

The cumulonimbus in its mature stage (D) develops a flat "anvil" top that usually spreads out into the storm path. By observing this cirruslike spread, you can forecast the storm's direction. When an anvil top approaches you it spreads overhead like a cobwebbed ceiling, and you know then that it is only a matter of less than a half-hour before the wind shift and downpour.

The Army's Thunderstorm Project once tried

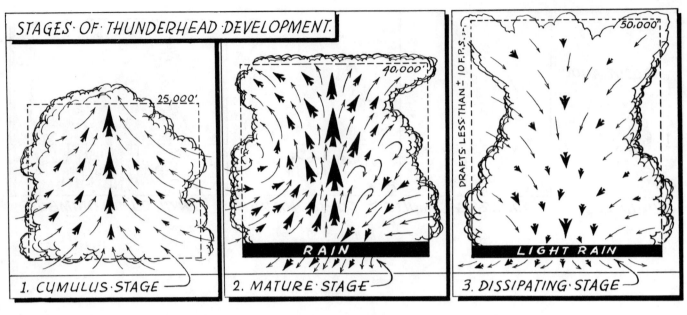

Drawing 61

to settle the question of what goes on inside a thunderhead. Wings had been ripped from bombers and heavy airliners had been turned upside down by thunderheads. Pilots claimed that hurricane-force updrafts and downdrafts existed inside, while scientists estimated the updrafts at only a few miles an hour and completely doubted the powerful downdraft theory. Drawing 61 shows what the Army project's pilotless "drones" and free balloons found out about the thermal thunderstorm's anatomy — that (1) it first built up a large updraft, being fed from the sides (cumulus stage); a downdraft (2) was circulated in the mature stage; and (3) a final dissipating stage consisted entirely of downdrafts. Notice the top height has grown from 25,000 feet to 50,000 feet before dissipation has taken over. The anvil top seems to forecast this last stage. This type of thunderhead is so concentrated, I might note, that the airliner may easily fly around it and thus avoid the turbulence.

Much research has been done on thunderstorm anatomy, using radar. By setting metallic balloons loose inside all parts of a storm their actions may be watched by radar, giving ac-

curate indication of updrafts and downdrafts. The thunderhead itself is readily reflected on the radarscope because, unlike other clouds which have tiny droplets of moisture with very little reflective quality, the cumulonimbus has large droplets and heavy reflective layers of ice, snow, and rain. Radar, of course, is an electrical "echo-machine" which bounces back on impulse only where there is something solid enough to bounce it back. Drawing 62 shows how a cold front reveals a strong echo on a radar screen, making the radar a fine short-range storm forecaster. Each ring may indicate five, ten, or more miles of distance. The radarscope shown here warns of a cold front with two thunderheads about fifteen miles away (three five-mile rings).

It is difficult to describe a thunderhead without including lightning, for it is only within these aerial machines of violent updrafts that the atmosphere's electrical charges become scattered and in a position to equalize themselves again by discharging from one area to another.

First of all, lightning is the child of violent updrafts. Warm sultry air, when thrown aloft

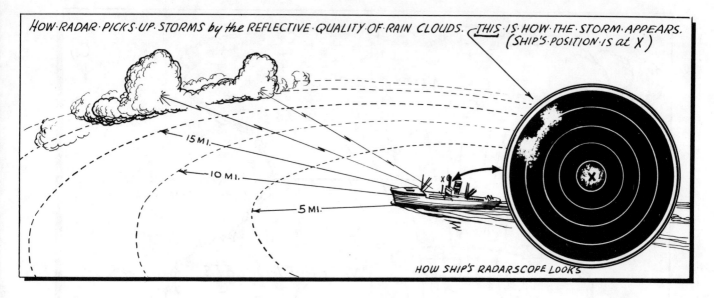

Drawing 62

into cold heights too quickly to dissipate its electrical differences will overcharge its cloud-form slowly, yet discharge it with an instantaneous bang. The cumulonimbus or thunderhead cloud is always the powerhouse. Watch for it looming over the horizon from the west or northwest (because thunderheads usually move eastward). In the temperate zones,

lightning from anywhere but the west or northwest, remember, will most likely pass you by.

You've often heard of timing thunder to tell how far away the lightning occurred, but have probably forgotten the formula. As Drawing 63 shows, simply count the interval between flash and report in seconds, then multiply by ⅕ to get the answer in miles.

Drawing 63

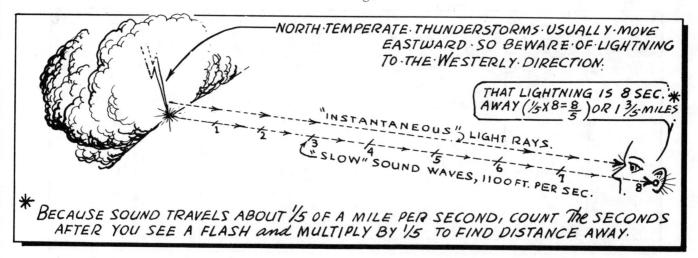

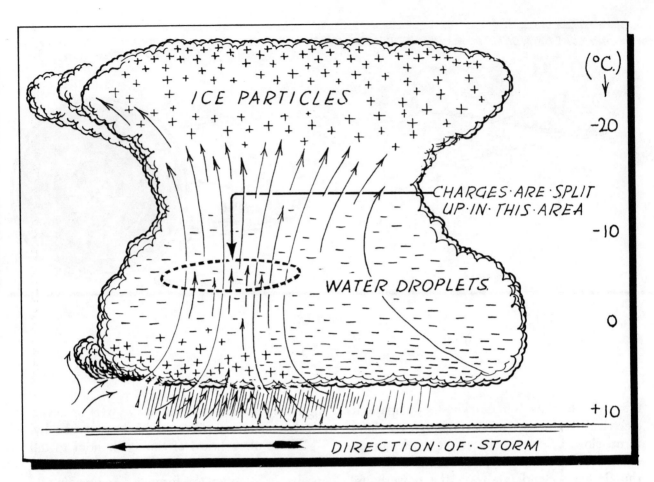

Drawing 64

Drawing 64 shows a schematic diagram of electrical distribution in a thundercloud. The currents within a thunderhead are so gusty that the raindrops are repeatedly broken into smaller drops. Each time this occurs, the nega-tive and positive electricity will be separated; the air takes up the negative current and the raindrop takes up a positive charge. By repeated splitting up of the drops, enormous electrical charges are made available within

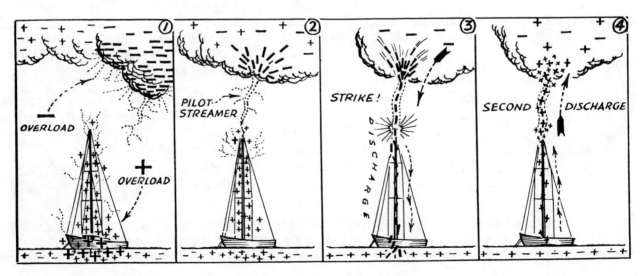

Drawing 65

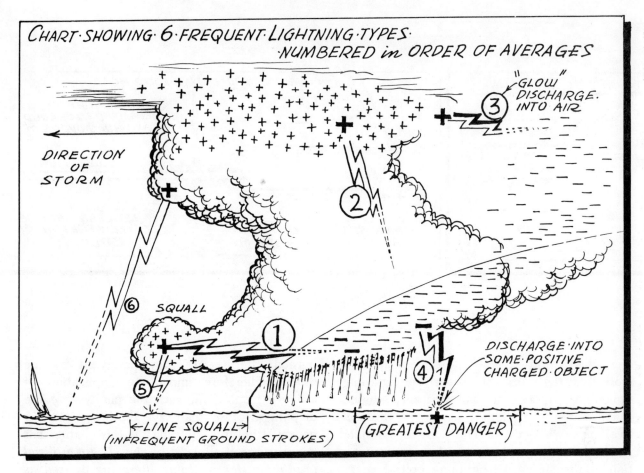

CHART·SHOWING·6·FREQUENT·LIGHTNING·TYPES·
·NUMBERED in ORDER OF AVERAGES

"GLOW" DISCHARGE. INTO AIR

DIRECTION OF STORM

SQUALL

DISCHARGE·INTO SOME·POSITIVE CHARGED·OBJECT

←LINE SQUALL→ (INFREQUENT GROUND STROKES)

(GREATEST DANGER)

Drawing 66

the cloud. Since the air ascends more rapidly than the drops that it breaks up, it follows that part of the cloud where updrafts abound will be positive, while the rest will be negative or neutral.

I know that a tall ship's mast aiming at a thundercloud is an ominous sight, but at 4000 feet such a target is of much less importance than it seems from shipboard. It will survive lightning far better than a house on a hill. Besides, the wind and waves accompanying a cumulonimbus, which might not be as frightening as a lightning bolt, are far more dangerous to the sailor. Chances are that you'll never be struck.

It all happens in a twinkling of an eye, but the lightning bolt involves the creation of oppositely charged areas, an introductory pilot streamer, and a series of rapid exchanges of current. Drawing 65 shows that a tall-masted boat, when struck, really strikes the cloud

instead of being struck, by contacting the cloud's streamer and emptying the overcharge into itself. Once contact has been made and the cloud has discharged into the earthly object, surrounding clouds may join in and empty themselves one after the other, first through the original cloud, then through the bolt channel. Thus one bolt can consist of several impulses, the stroke channel being used over and over again, a score of times in the fraction of a second. A quick eye can often detect several impulses in a large lightning bolt. Drawing 66 shows the various kinds of discharge that are possible, numbered in their average occurrences. Notice that the uprush of air pushes the positive charge aloft, while the falling rain concentrates a negative charge in the cloud base.

So-called "heat lightning" is just plain lightning that is occurring too far away for you to hear its thunder. Thunder cannot be heard

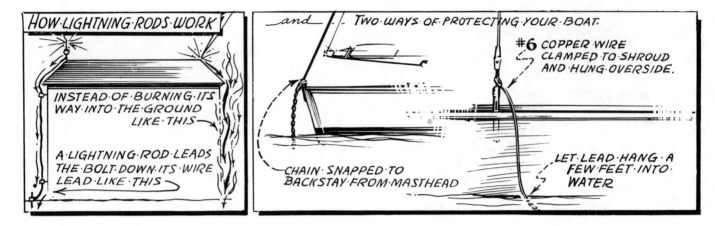

Drawing 67

more than twenty-five miles away, usually not more than ten miles. Small flares of lightning sometimes happen with no apparent thunder. Their power is negligible, having no destructive force whatsoever. The noise of thunder results from the sudden expansion and contraction of the air as the lightning bolts heat it. Thunder is similar to the expansion and contraction of air at the muzzle of a gun when it is discharged. Echoes from the initial explosive discharge continue for a half minute or more, constituting the rumbling of thunder.

A boat, if alone on a flat stretch of water, is an invitation to the heavenly discharge, but the chance that she will be struck is about one for every hundred years of such exposure. The chance that a bolt might take a personal interest in you is close to one in a million.

If the craft has a very tall mast the chances are greater, but the heavy metal stays make perfect lightning-rod leaders toward the water. If you would like to make them real leaders you could snap short lengths of cable to each one, as shown in Drawing 67, allowing them to enter the water. But if land is near, your boat is not as exposed as you think. Only when well at sea need you worry.

Lightning does strike water, so swimming should be avoided. This brings up something of importance. Seldom are struck swimmers

burned. Rather are they paralyzed by the shock. Therefore immediate application of artificial respiration, until the paralysis of the diaphragm ceases, can save the life of many a person struck by lightning. If this chapter has any message at all, let it be this: *Learn artificial respiration, for lightning lifesaving as well as for first aid in drowning.*

The most dangerous places to be during a lightning storm are in the bathtub, between two metal objects such as the boat engine and a metal mast, or under a large tree. Boats are struck, but the death list is probably no higher than for people struck in houses. There is no reason whatever for a sailor worrying about it. A convertible automobile is an invitation to danger, but an all-metal car becomes a faraday cage which surrounds you with absolute safety. All-metal airplanes are also safe vessels; they are very frequently struck without any damage being done to them.

It is commonly observed that the higher the clouds, the lower the proportion of strokes to the ground. This is because the overcharged cloud first sends down a pilot streamer seeking contact with a discharge point. A very tall object may send a pilot streamer upward toward the cloud after the manner of a St. Elmo's light discharge, before lightning contact is made. But it is assumed an average

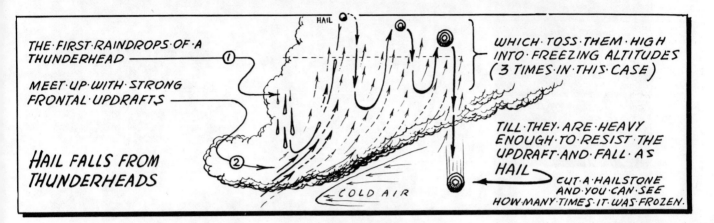

THE·FIRST·RAINDROPS·OF·A THUNDERHEAD ——— ①

MEET·UP·WITH·STRONG FRONTAL·UPDRAFTS ———

HAIL FALLS FROM THUNDERHEADS ②

HAIL

WHICH·TOSS·THEM·HIGH INTO·FREEZING·ALTITUDES (3 TIMES·IN·THIS·CASE)

TILL·THEY·ARE·HEAVY ENOUGH·TO·RESIST·THE UPDRAFT·AND·FALL·AS HAIL

CUT·A·HAILSTONE AND·YOU·CAN·SEE HOW·MANY·TIMES·IT·WAS·FROZEN.

COLD AIR

Drawing 68

mast would not be sufficiently tall to so attract lightning. It was found that only two of fifty-two strokes to the Empire State Building were known to be initiated by downward leaders.

Hail, too, is a child of the cumulonimbus. Perhaps you've noticed that the first drops of a thunderstorm are always the biggest. The reason is simply that only the heaviest drops can fall through the powerful storm updraft. In fact many drops are carried aloft and quick-frozen into hail. Drawing 68 shows how hail is formed when the updraft is particularly strong. Hail must be carried aloft several times and re-frozen to larger size before it is heavy enough to fall through the violent upward winds.

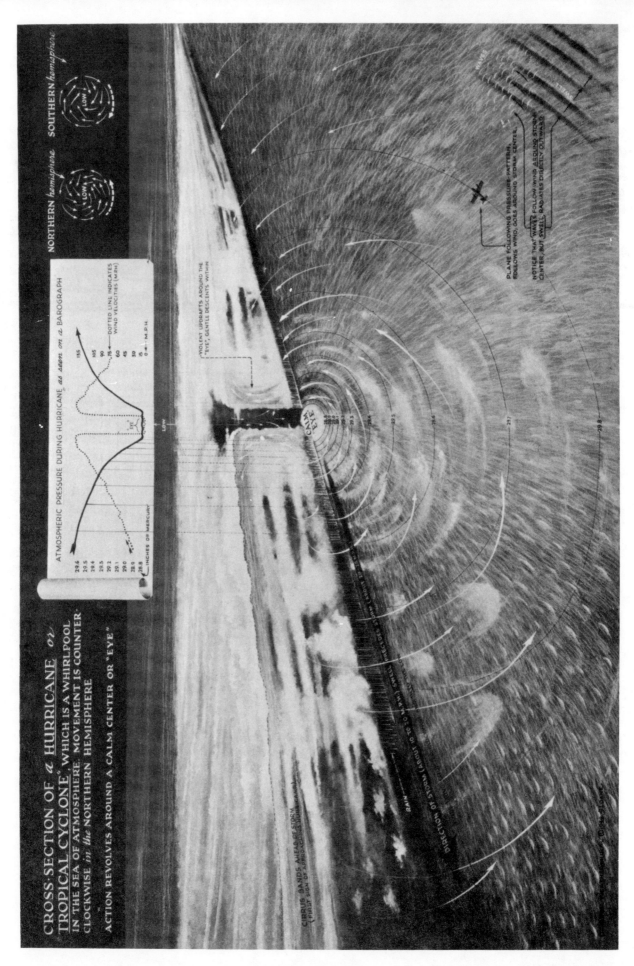

Drawing 69

13 WINDS THAT DO NO GOOD

For I fear a hurricane.
Last night, the moon had a golden ring,
And to-night no moon we see!
— LONGFELLOW

It's an ill wind, they say, that blows no good. I know of a bakery firm that hires its own meteorologist to predict the rainy and windy days so that the plant may prepare to bake fewer loaves of bread on such days. Housewives, it appears, will not brave the weather; they prefer to bake at home during the bad days; leftover, spoiled loaves of bread can amount to thousands of dollars. These bad days are a problem for the baker, but they are a boon to the flour mills and the gas companies that help to make those homemade loaves. But there really are ill winds that are just good for nothing. Take, for example, the hurricane.

Always a thriller for the scientific writer, the hurricane probably has had more articles and books written about it than any other weather phenomenon. Yet if someone asks you what a hurricane is, can you tell him? It is much more than a big wind, you know. It is a compact piece of atmospheric machinery, made in several inconvenient sizes, and designed to do an expert job of destruction during its destined course. In fact, hurricanes are so constructed that you could cut any one of them in half like an apple and find the same sort of anatomy. I have done just that in Drawing 69, which is a gigantic cut-through the center, or eye, of a hurricane.

Called "typhoons" in East Asia and "hurricanes" in the West Indies, these storms are more correctly known as TROPICAL CYCLONES. "Cyclone" is, no doubt, the most misunderstood word in the layman's meteorological vocabulary. If I said that yesterday's mild drizzle was the result of a cyclone, you would probably pick up the paper and look for the casualty reports from some nearby storm. Yet any little, rainy low-pressure area is really a cyclone. The word comes from the Greek *kyklos,* meaning a circle, and the dictionary says a cyclone is nothing other than "a wind blowing circularly," or "a circular wind system."

On your daily weather map you will see any number of highs and lows. Each high is an ANTICYCLONE and each low is a CYCLONE. This simply means that in the Northern Hemisphere the winds blow clockwise around one (the high) and counterclockwise around the other (the low).

Cyclones and anticyclones travel from two hundred to five hundred miles a day in summer and from five hundred to seven hundred miles a day during winter. Lows or cyclones move faster than highs or anticyclones, but both follow more or less defined paths. Drawing 70 shows the average paths of these circular weather machines. The more clearly defined the high or low, the more it will keep to the paths shown in this drawing. Try plotting the course of some high or low from your weather map, using this drawing as a guide, and see how close your forecast will be.

Most people confuse the word "cyclone" with

CHARACTERISTIC HIGHS and CHARACTERISTIC LOWS.

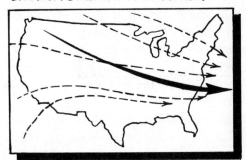

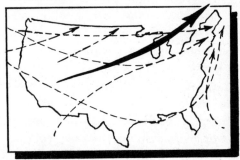

Drawing 70

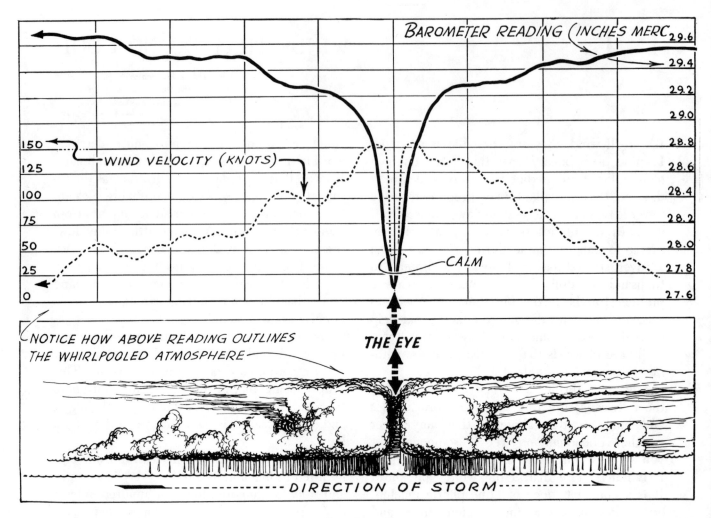

Drawing 71

TORNADO (twister) or with TROPICAL CYCLONE (hurricane). The dread tropical cyclone is a simple cyclone, but, born in the heat of the tropics, instead of wearing itself out by friction, it has fed upon the latent heat associated with the warm, flat stretches of water and there has become an uncontrollable global whirlpool on a rampage. When you explain this to a youngster, you might fill the tub with water, then take the stopper out; let him observe the whirlpool and then tell him a hurricane is a whirlpool in the sea of the air. If he wants to know how the storm goes only ten miles an hour, yet has winds over a hundred miles an hour, start your portable victrola. Show him how you may walk about from room to room slowly or even stop completely, yet the record always goes around steadily and just

as fast. That is exactly how the hurricane works.

The complete barometer readings during a hurricane are of great interest, but being a diagram of something that has already happened, there is not too great forecast value in them. You have no doubt seen many barograph readings such as Drawing 71 portrays. Every yacht club has them framed or stowed away somewhere. An interesting feature in them is that the barographic line actually outlines the anatomy of the atmosphere's density; it draws a pictorial slice through a whirlpool and makes a sort of cutaway drawing of the storm.

The eye of the hurricane might average from three to fifteen miles across; because the whole storm revolves around it, this area is calm. The rain there may cease and the sky may clear overhead almost completely. If the eye

80

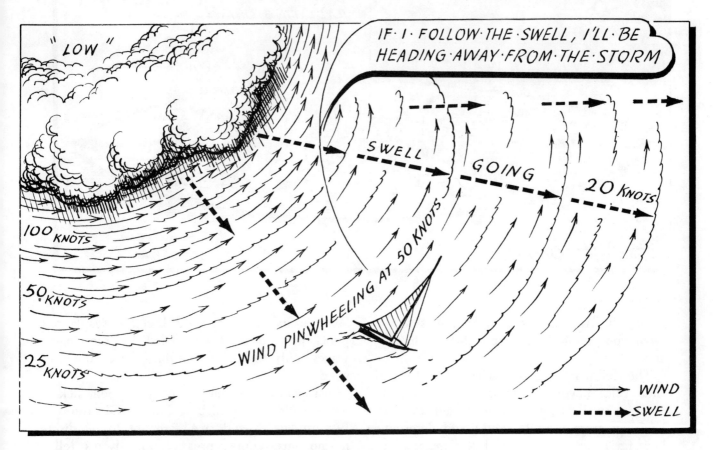

Drawing 72

passed directly over you, you would experience this calm, but the minute the eye went on its way the wind would begin again, this time in the opposite direction, or from the opposite side of the aerial whirlpool. This explains mysterious accounts of trees that have been blown down and in a few moments blown upright again during the same storm.

Notice in the cutaway back in Drawing 69 how the upper clouds mushroom outward into a flat ceiling of cirroform. This sheet of chaotic and weblike cloud is ample warning of winds to come. Even more positive a warning is the sea swell that radiates outward from the storm center. A hurricane may loaf along or stand still, yet the swells radiate outward at considerable speed. Drawing 72 shows the relationship between swell and storm. This illustration shows a swell of twenty-five knots preceding a storm whose center is moving along at

only ten knots. Even if it stood still, the swell would continue to flow outward at about the same speed.

Every sailor knows SWELL when he sees it, but ask him for a definition and words begin to come hard. To start with, swell is not a wave. Waves are wind ruffles, whereas swells are caused by some disturbance. Drawing 73 shows a pond with the wind making a solid pattern of waves, all going in one direction — the direction of the wind. *Kerplop!* goes a stone right in the middle of our wind pattern and swells immediately radiate outward from it, weaving right through the waves. Off to the right of the drawing, the waves and swell are both moving in the same direction, but at the left — where you see the schematic cross-section slice — waves and swell are moving in opposite directions. The bigger the stone, the bigger the ripples; the bigger the hurricane the bigger

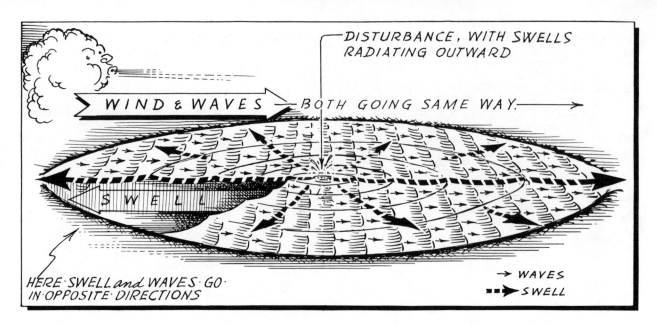

Drawing 73

the swell. And always at right angles to the swell you can look for some sort of disturbance.

The fellows with the scientific data and slide rules have even figured out a way to measure swell (height is from trough to crest, length is from crest to crest) and determine how far away the storm is. Not many of us are really going out to measure the wet stuff, but Drawing 74 gives you an idea of the mathematics involved, showing how a swell loses one third of its height every time it travels as many miles as its length is in feet.

Airmen who are not swell-conscious should not fly seaplanes, for many a man has landed into ten-inch waves only to find that they are running up and down ten-foot swells. That's bad. When swells run at right angles to wind waves, the sunlight that gives shadow to the waves will naturally run parallel to the swell and therefore not reveal it. Then again, swell

being no indication of wind direction, seaplane pilots have often been fooled by the "big waves" only to land in a calm or even downwind.

Seasickness (which is really motion sickness) could very well be called "swell jitters." Because waves and swell are apt to be disharmonious, your senses cannot always tell when you are going up and when you are going down. In this case your body will not "ride" the waves well and your stomach muscles are apt to relax when they are supposed to tighten. Finally they give up in disgust or become hysterical over the many indecisions. Motion sickness is really a nervous breakdown of the stomach.

Tornadoes are often called cyclones and hurricanes. Actually they are concentrated twisters, short-lived but most vicious of all. They are the most compact low-pressure machine in the whole atmosphere. Few of us connect pressure

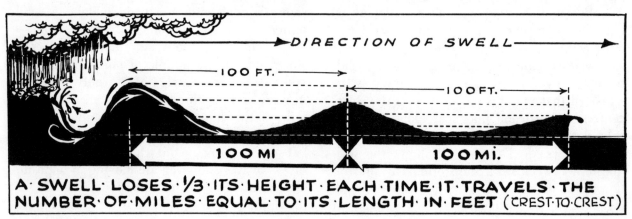

A SWELL LOSES 1/3 ITS HEIGHT EACH TIME IT TRAVELS THE NUMBER OF MILES EQUAL TO ITS LENGTH IN FEET (CREST-TO-CREST)

Drawing 74

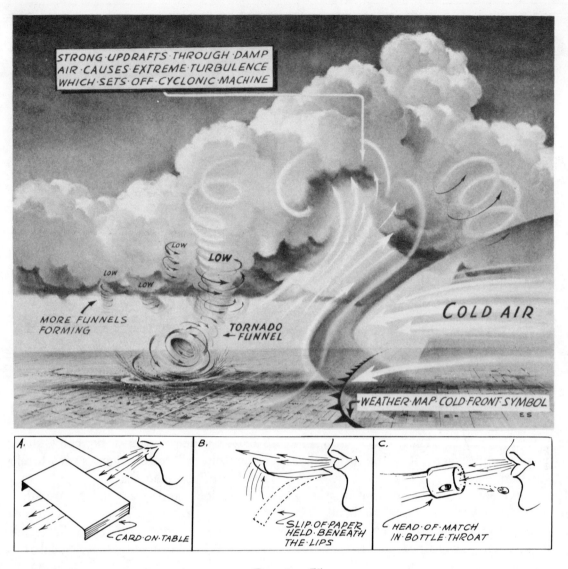

STRONG·UPDRAFTS·THROUGH·DAMP AIR·CAUSES·EXTREME·TURBULENCE WHICH·SETS·OFF·CYCLONIC·MACHINE

LOW

LOW

LOW

LOW

LOW

MORE FUNNELS FORMING

TORNADO FUNNEL

COLD AIR

WEATHER·MAP·COLD·FRONT·SYMBOL

A. CARD·ON·TABLE

B. SLIP·OF·PAPER HELD·BENEATH THE·LIPS

C. HEAD·OF·MATCH IN·BOTTLE·THROAT

Drawing 75

with wind, yet the two are closely associated. The most interesting thing about cyclones, hurricanes, and tornadoes is the low pressure that feeds their machinery. Most people think that when a tornado passes over a house it blows it down; actually, it *sucks* it down. The sudden low pressure on the outside of the house leaves normal high pressure inside, enough to blow the house outward. Probably you have seen pictures of cattle untouched within a barn that has been blown outward from a tornado. Automobile tires in the path of such low pressure will burst outward, and watches, bottled goods, or any air-filled articles will explode outward.

You'd think that a fast stream of air would cause a great deal of outward pressure, but it doesn't. If you suspend two ping-pong balls close together and then blow between them,

they don't blow apart. Believe it or not, they are pulled together! Or try the experiments shown with Drawing 75. Blow beneath a folded card (A) and see it hug the surface; you'd think it would blow away. Blow on top of a piece of paper that you hold under your mouth and see it curl upward instead of away (B). Place the head of a match in the throat of a bottle and try to blow it the rest of the way in (C); it will pop right out into your face!

The most awesome weather sight at sea, yet the least understood, is a waterspout. Most sailors think it is a column of water sucked up from the sea. But if there is water within the spout at all, it is fresh water and not sea water. When a waterspout ceases, a torrent of sea water does not fall back into the sea; the

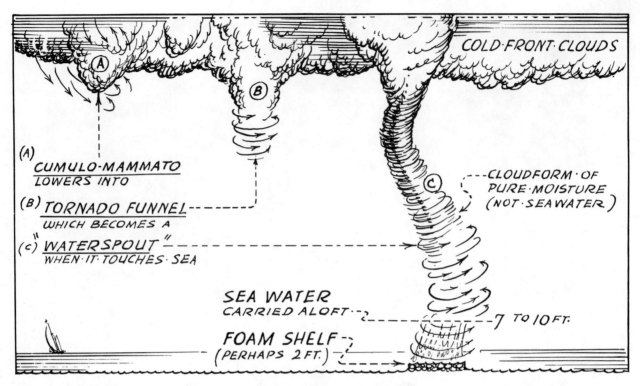

COLD·FRONT·CLOUDS

(A) CUMULO-MAMMATO
LOWERS INTO

(B) TORNADO FUNNEL
WHICH BECOMES A

(C) "WATERSPOUT"
WHEN·IT·TOUCHES·SEA

---CLOUDFORM·OF
PURE·MOISTURE
(NOT·SEAWATER)

SEA WATER
CARRIED ALOFT

7 TO 10 FT.

FOAM SHELF
(PERHAPS 2 FT.)

Drawing 76

funnel simply passes silently back into the atmosphere from where it came originally. It's just a dark cloud.

The waterspout is a cloud that marks a tornado whirlpool in the sea of air beneath a line squall or cumulonimbus. The winds are around and not upward, as you may think. When a tornado vortex occurs over the water, its low-pressure core may suck sea water eight to ten feet upward, but this is very unusual. With an average diameter of twenty to sixty feet, these seagoing tornadoes last for about ten minutes and actually do very little damage. Thousands occur yearly.

Drawing 76 shows the characteristic MAMMATO CLOUDS (A) that mark the bottom of an average thunderhead or line squall. MAMMATUS is a descriptive term applicable to clouds having lower surfaces that hang downward like great breasts or pouches. Thought to be the result of downdrafts, these lumps have never been completely studied and it is my opinion that whirlpool effects often occur within them. At least it seems that many tornadoes are a continuation of mammato forms (B), which finally contact the earth (C) and make a complete machine. Probably the most famous waterspout is in Winslow Homer's painting, "The Gulf

Stream" which shows a typical Gulf Stream waterspout where the cloud seems to elongate and "drip" into the sea.

Tornadoes and waterspouts usually move parallel with a squall line traveling east or northeast at from twenty to fifty miles an hour. While every meteorological textbook defines a "waterspout" as "a tornado at sea," there seems to be no written mention of why the land storm often lasts for as long as an hour while the seaspout version averages five or ten minutes.

Although very rare, aerial whirlpools, such as those that whisk newspapers around a windy street, will occur over open water with enough force to condense a cloud from the water level instead of from the storm cloud above. These vortexes are similar to the "dust-devils" seen whirling in ten- to fifty-foot columns over dry deserts.

According to old legends, tornadoes and waterspouts can be broken by firing a gun into them. Could a cloud be broken by firing at it? The legends can be marked off as inaccurate folklore, probably the result of a waterspout having disappeared at the very moment a gun happened to be fired at it.

Drawing 77

14

ATMOSPHERIC ANTICS

> *. . . Sometimes I'd divide*
> *And burn in many places; on the topmast,*
> *The yards and bowsprit, would I flame distinctly,*
> *Then meet and join. . . .*
> — SHAKESPEARE

A sailor with Columbus once wrote, "And at the height of this foule weather the storme did settle upon our vessel in strange manner. A ghostly flame danced among our sails and later stayed like candle lights to burn brightly from the masts." This eerie phenomenon called St. Elmo's light occurs as often on land as it does on sea, but the loneliness and darkness of night on the water, along with the convenient playground of masts and spars at fair height from the ground, have helped to make it one of the haunting legends of the sea. Get a few old salts talking about the supernatural and you'll always hear a few words about St. Elmo's light.

In reality a "brush discharge" or "corona discharge," St. Elmo's light was really unmasked and researched in all-weather airplane flights during the war. It was a frequent occurrence during Atlantic flights, when entire wings and protruding parts of airplanes were at times enveloped in this orange and bluish light. Propellers often became pinwheels of flame so bright that the uninitiated would be prepared to jump from the "burning plane." Because the occurrence of corona discharge is more frequent in aircraft than on surface vessels, we will examine St. Elmo's light by imagining ourselves on a "hot" plane.

EVAPORATION PRECIPITATION LOADS VESSEL WITH UNEVEN CHARGE AS IT SAILS THROUGH POSITIVE CHARGED FOG PATCHES

..VESSEL IS NOW UNEVENLY CHARGED AS IT SAILS INTO THIS NEGATIVE ATMOSPHERE—....

..VESSEL DISCHARGES ITS UNEVEN LOAD INTO SURROUNDING AIR AS CORONA DISCHARGE OR ST. ELMO'S LIGHT.

Drawing 78

The weather is closing in and there are scurries of snow. The radio is noisy with atmospheric interference. This crackling, caused by the ship's passing through clouds overladen with positive current, may finally render the radio useless. Your ship, you see, is collecting potential faster than it can dissipate it through normal leakage. The process is very similar to that which occurs when you walk over a thick rug during a crisp winter day: you collect current that will jump from your fingertip whenever you come in contact with a light switch or person that can use the overload. Your plane, too, bursting with the overload which now is spilling over with visible glow, is ready to discharge into the nearest cloud which is low in positive current. The weather-wise pilot will know enough to wear dark glasses and wait for the lightning-bolt discharge, which is loud and scary but perfectly harmless. Such is the capering of St. Elmo's light aloft; but a boat at sea may also sail through fog or snow patches, picking up unequal current and glowing wherever it discharges the overload into the surrounding atmosphere (see Drawing 78).

Phosphorescent water is not a phenomenon of St. Elmo's light, although the atmosphere and oxygen mechanics is involved. Most of us have been swimming during a rain when each raindrop hit the water's surface with a little spar-kling light.

Many seamen swear that phosphorescent sea is caused by minute jellyfish being turned upon their backs. That, of course, is far-fetched. All of us have seen the glow of jellyfish when they are walked upon or struck after being cast up on shore. Jellyfish do secrete bacteria which glow during exudation, causing a phosphorescent effect, but jellyfish themselves do not cause the phenomenon. The crest of a wave, or any agitation which might throw active water into a spray that mingles with atmosphere, will cause sufficient oxidation to give the startling and beautiful effect of phosphorescent sea.

Many of the weird "spook lights" that occur are explained simply. When open burials were common or rotten pine coffins were envolved, the low pressure of bad weather often loosed from decaying bodies the phosphorus which floated in the damp air of graveyards. Recently someone found out that wintergreen Life Saver candy, if broken in a pitch-black room, made a tiny spark; this discovery amused the children no end and, I guess, sold a lot of wintergreens.

Few of us have missed the thrill of seeing "northern lights" or the aurora borealis. In reality this magnificent nighttime display does not originate from the northern seas or from the reflection of sun or polar ice—as often supposed

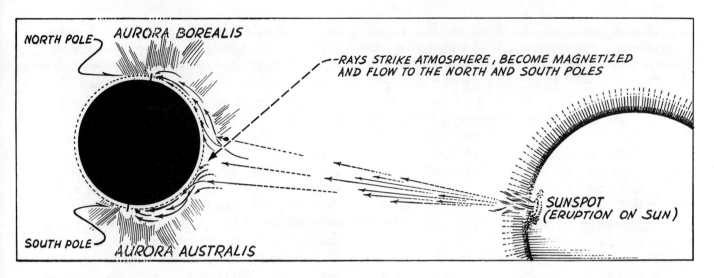

Drawing 79

— but directly from the sun. It occurs beyond the stratosphere, in the outer stretches of atmosphere called the ionosphere, about seventy miles up. Whenever the sun has a volcanic eruption (as evidenced by a large sunspot) great streams of electrified particles rocket through space toward the earth at terrific speed, colliding with the rarefied gases of the upper atmosphere and making a disturbance which blazes into a brilliant battleground of fire and flashes. Actually there is always an overload of electrified particles sent to us, but after the ninety-three million miles and twenty-four hours between the sun and the earth, they have become very much affected by our world's magnetic field. Instead of penetrating any part of our air then, they flow toward the regions of the North and South Magnetic Poles (Drawing 79) where the heavens glow eternally with solar overcharge. The aurora at the northern magnetic field is called AURORA BOREALIS, the one at the southern field AURORA AUSTRALIS. Auroras have been said by sailors to indicate good weather, and there is at certain times some truth in this. When a great mass of polar air comes in, visibility is keen through the dry cold atmosphere, so that auroral lights become brighter. Polar air, of course, means a weather purge and a few days of crisp good weather.

Possibly the most widely publicized atmospheric antics have been our own doing, the experimental research into "man-made rain."

First of all, I will be cautious and state that only God can *make* rain. The so-called "rainmakers" simply increase precipitation. Of course, a great deal of rain falls from the clouds that never reaches the earth, as it evaporates quickly back into the atmosphere. In flying through clouds it is observed that raindrops spatter the windshield even on a fine day. The idea is to make such rainfall heavier and lasting enough to reach the earth. It has been established that we can increase such light precipitation by CLOUD SEEDING. Of course, first there must be a cloud and the rain material must be there to "seed."

We will take as an example a cumulus cloud formed by rising currents which constantly lift warm moisture-laden air far above the sun-warmed earth into regions where it is winter all the year. Clouds are composed of water droplets formed by cooling and condensation. These droplets ordinarily are too small to fall as rain and are kept aloft by the updrafts. At the center of the cloud the draft is strongest, and it is here that water droplets are lifted to heights where the temperature is below 32° Fahrenheit.

Strangely enough, the droplets in the top

of this cauliflowerlike cloud do not freeze, although the temperature is well below the freezing point. This phenomenon is known as "supercooling." If we could get all these super-cooled droplets to freeze, grow to snowflake size, and fall (instead of constantly being kept aloft by the updraft), they would drop earth-ward through warmer air and melt into rain. This we now are able to do and the process is called "cloud seeding."

In Drawing 80, Figure 1 shows a cloud-seed-ing operation where ice pellets are dropped into a slightly raining or at least a growing rain cloud. The sequence of supercooled droplets to ice crystals to snowflakes to rain can be ob-served.

As shown in Figure 2, when a dry ice pellet is dropped through a supercooled cloudform, droplets close to the falling ice are chilled below the critical 40° Fahrenheit and ice crystals are formed. These crystals disperse through the turbulent air of the cloudform and cause snow, and by making the cloud snow heav-ily we get rain. It is melted snow, but it is rain to us below.

The term "cloud seeding" was introduced by the General Electric Research Laboratories and since the early experiments we have found that minute silver-iodide smoke crystals, which are similar in construction to ice crystals, will also serve as nuclei. Because smoke rises, it is easier to send crystals aloft than it is to fly up over the cloud and drop material into it. Silver iodide in solid form or in solution is fed into a generator to windward of a likely-looking cloud. The generator heats it to about 1500° Centigrade, at which point it becomes vaporized. At this point it is thrown out into the surrounding cooler at-mosphere as an almost invisible smoke of micro-scopic-sized smoke crystals. About twenty tril-lion smoke crystals a second are produced by a smoke generator, and one milligram of silver iodide is enough to seed one cubic mile of cloudy air.

Figure 3 shows a smoke generator at work. A cloud of likely size and height is spotted to the lee of a fair wind and the forced draft of silver iodide smoke is begun (A). Picked up by the cloud's natural updraft (all cumulus clouds, as we have shown, have updrafts be-neath them), the smoke ascends into the upper cloud where ice crystals are formed (B). The formation of snow occurs (C); and when the flakes grow in size they fall to lower and warmer levels, where they melt into rain (D).

One might reason that a cloud is like a giant watering pot and that if its contents are emptied all at once in one spot, we might thereby deprive the people downwind of their rightful rain. But available evidence indicates that precipitation downwind from the area of increased rainfall is not appreciably les-sened. The cloudform is not drained but usually becomes larger, and the lateral mixing with neighboring air masses more than makes up for the amount of rainfall squeezed out by man. Nevertheless, lawsuits by bands of farmers suing for "rain robbery" already amount to many millions of dollars.

Because of local variations in rainfall it is nearly impossible to evaluate cloud-seeding operations, but in many instances "rainmaking" has proved its worth, particularly in the high elevations of the mountainous West. As for future developments, we shall see what we shall see. I am pessimistic.

Man cannot compete with Nature's atmos-pheric antics when it comes to color. It is not only one of our hackneyed expressions that "a sunset is a picture no artist can paint"; it's a known fact. Light is so transparent and paints are so opaque in quality that direct sunlight, even when it shines through the translucence of dust and haze, is impossible to reproduce. Sunlit clouds around the sunset become pos-sible and very interesting subjects — and, by the way, much more exciting than the sunset itself. The most magnificent "sunsets" are not in the west at all, but in the east! When you are in the open and viewing the sun going down, do watch the deep and sullen clouds on the op-posite eastern horizon as they reflect the set-ting western light. The changing colors are as thrilling as a symphony. You will also hear about "unusual" sunsets at various places, but you can discount many of them as having oc-curred on occasions when the viewer was on

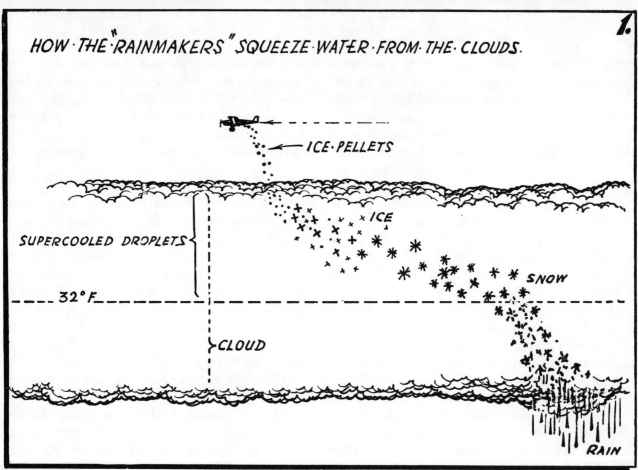

HOW·THE·"RAINMAKERS"·SQUEEZE·WATER·FROM·THE·CLOUDS.

1.

ICE·PELLETS

SUPERCOOLED·DROPLETS

ICE

32°F.

SNOW

CLOUD

RAIN

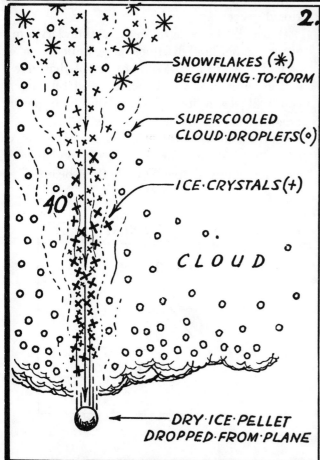

2.

SNOWFLAKES (✳)
BEGINNING·TO·FORM

SUPERCOOLED
CLOUD·DROPLETS (○)

ICE·CRYSTALS (+)

40°

CLOUD

DRY·ICE·PELLET
DROPPED·FROM·PLANE

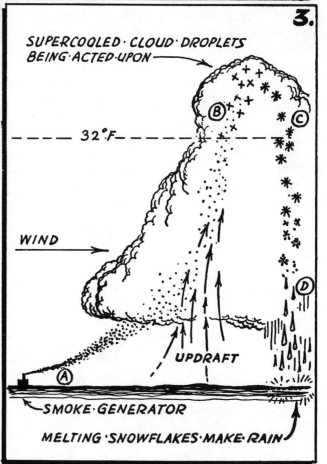

3.

SUPERCOOLED·CLOUD·DROPLETS
BEING·ACTED·UPON

B   C

32°F.

WIND

D

UPDRAFT

A

SMOKE·GENERATOR

MELTING·SNOWFLAKES·MAKE·RAIN

Drawing 80

vacation or relaxed enough to find the time to look upward and behold what goes on constantly, but what was unnoticed before. Some of the most wonderful sunsets occur right in New York City or around large towns, because the sun's light shining through dusty air creates hues that are close to deep purple and geranium lake.

You will remember our discussion about snow not really being white. Well, we can continue that theme by remarking that the sky is not really blue. Space is jet black and air is really colorless, but the many particles of air refract the light of the sun so completely that they divide sunlight into its true body of colors and we see color more than light. Try this refraction business with a glass of water (as shown in Drawing 81) and you will find that sunlight is not only light but color too. Notice that the predominant color (because it refracts most easily) is blue. All the rest of the colors are in the sky too, but there is so much blue that it crowds the other colors out. We see only blue and say, "The sky is blue." Dust refracts red, which causes things near the horizon to appear redder, such as the far clouds, the setting sun, or the moon. But high above, where the air is dust-free, the sky begins to be a deeper blue — as Southey described it, "Blue, darkly, deeply, beautifully blue." Above the troposphere, the sky is gun-metal-blue; and presently it becomes the blackness of stellar space.

The formation of a rainbow depends upon the passage of light through water droplets much in the same manner of our glass-of-water demonstration. Because the sun must be less than forty-two degrees above the horizon, you will not see a noonday rainbow except in higher latitudes. There is a saying:
A rainbow in the morning, shepherds take warning;
A rainbow at night is the shepherd's delight.

Which is quite logical, when you observe that weather patterns usually move from the west to the east. If you see a rainbow reflected by the morning sun you will be looking at moist air toward the west that will later reach you. But if you see a rainbow reflected by a late-in-the-day sun, you will be seeing it against the rain backdrop that is already on its way eastward — and good weather is with you. A jingle more to the sailor's liking is:
Rainbow to windward, foul fall the day;
Rainbow to leeward, damp runs away.

The justification of this is that, if the rainbow is to windward, the shower is approaching, while if it appears to leeward, no rain can come from that moist curtain because it is already receding.

It usually takes a rainbow, a thunderstorm, or some other kind of atmospheric antic to make us look upward and take note; but if that gives us the habit, it is worth while. And I'll wager you will see a lot up there that you never dreamed of. So try it if possible.

As the weather-wise Zuñi Indians have a way of saying, "With your eyes in the sky, in old age may you walk lively in a path of beauty."

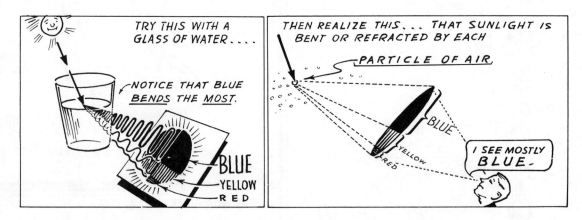

Drawing 81